THE HERITAGE OF INDIA SERIES (5)

PSALMS OF MARATHA SAINTS

THE HERITAGE OF INDIA SERIES (5)

PSALMS OF MARATHA SAINTS

One Hundred and Eight Hymns
translated from the Marathi

BY

NICOL MACNICOL, M. A., D. LITT.

GYAN

Published by

GYAN

Gyan Publishing House
5, Ansari Road
Daryaganj, New Delhi-110002
Phone: 011-47034999, 9811692060
E-mail: books@gyanbooks.com

Distribution Network
gyanbooks.com
India, USA, Canada, UK, Australia, France

ISBN: 978-81-212-8273-4 (PB)
First Published, 1919

2nd Impression 2023

Printed at: Gyan Press, Delhi.

THE HERITAGE OF INDIA SERIES (5); PSALMS OF MARATHA SAINTS
Translator: NICOL MACNICOL

VITHOBA OF PANDHARPUR.

THE HERITAGE OF INDIA

PSALMS OF MARĀTHĀ SAINTS

One Hundred and Eight Hymns
translated from the Marathi

BY

NICOL MACNICOL, M.A., D.LITT.
AUTHOR OF "INDIAN THEISM."

———

ASSOCIATION PRESS
5, RUSSELL STREET, CALCUTTA

LONDON: OXFORD UNIVERSITY PRESS
NEW YORK, TORONTO, MELBOURNE,
BOMBAY, AND MADRAS

A ROSARY
OF TULŚI BEADS
FOR
HELEN
AND
FRANCES.

PREFACE

THIS collection contains translations of one hundred and eight poems by some of the chief Vaiṣṇavite poets of the Marāṭhā country. The number seemed not inappropriate in view of the fact that there are one hundred and eight *tulsī* beads on the rosary worn by the Vaiṣṇavite devotee. Almost every one of these poems is a prayer, a cry of the saint to the god of his worship.

It has not been an easy matter to decide which poems should be selected for translation. Some have been chosen because they have a place in the regular worship of the devotees, as repeated daily by the *Vārkarīs* or adherents of the Paṇḍharpūr sect or sung in their *bhajans* or song services. But it was not easy to make a selection from so immense a body of literature as these poets have produced. I accordingly applied to Sir R. G. Bhandarkar with a request that he would assist me in making a choice, and he most kindly responded by furnishing me with a list of fifty *abhaṅgs* of Tukārām from those which he uses for his daily and weekly religious exercises. To anyone who knows Sir Ramkrishna Bhandarkar as not only a great Oriental scholar but the outstanding representative in India to-day of the ancient school of *bhakti*, the fact that these psalms minister nourishment to a spiritual life so beautiful and so sincere is in itself sufficient testimony to their religious value. For him, as for these saints, the life of the spirit is the only life livable, and fellowship with God its purpose and its goal. When one has known Sir Ramkrishna Bhandarkar the religion of these saints ceases to be of merely antiquarian interest. He is one of them still left among us for our reverence, and the strength and purity and tenderness of their devotion live again in him.

To other friends as well I have to acknowledge a deep debt of gratitude. I am very conscious of my own limitations as a student of the Marāṭhī language. I know how easy it is to misunderstand an allusion or to misinterpret a phrase in these poems. Ideas their authors are born to, and live by, we of the West grasp only with an effort. For that reason a foreigner's renderings must often be very imperfect. Mine would be much more imperfect even than they are, were it not for the kindness of two friends, Professor W. B. Patwardhan, of the Fergusson College, Poona, and Dr. V. A. Sukhtankar, of Indore. They have both read the proofs and have given me many criticisms and suggestions. I have to acknowledge with much gratitude this help. I have tried to improve the translations in many instances in accordance with their suggestions, but I am well aware that I have not by any means succeeded in removing all their defects. If, however, this little book awakens a wider interest in a little-known company of sincere singers and in their religion of passionate longing for the divine fellowship, I shall feel richly rewarded.

Poona, N. M.
August, 1919.

CONTENTS

		PAGE
	Introduction	11
	Note	34

JNĀNEŚVAR

I.	The Great Hearted	35
II.	The Rapture of devotion	36
III.	Aequanimitas	37
IV.	Truth	37
V.	"Cry Hari"	38
VI.	The Name	39
VII.	"There Needs Not a Propitious Hour" ..	40
VIII.	The Storehouse of Bliss	40

MUKTĀ BĀĪ

IX.	The Land of Topsy-turvy	41
X.	A Remonstrance	41

NĀMDEV

XI.	"Gone A e the Saints"	42
XII.	The Heart's Desire	42
XIII.	"O Haste and Come"	43
XIV.	A Vow	44
XV.	One Thing	44
XVI.	A Bitter Cry	44
XVII.	Seeking	45
XVIII.	"My Mother Thou"	46
XIX.	The Men of Faith	46
XX.	The Reign of Peace	47
XXI.	"Who Vasudev in All Can See" ..	47
XXII.	Illumination	48

JANĀBĀĪ

XXIII.	Pundlik	49
XXIV.	Grinding	49
XXV.	The Besetting God	50

PSALMS OF MARĀṬHĀ SAINTS

PAGE

EKANĀTH

XXVI.	God the Known and God the Unknown ..	51
XXVII.	The Ninefold Path of Bhakti	52
XXVIII.	The Scorner	53
XXIX.	Men's Reviling	54
XXX.	"God Dwells in All"	54
XXXI.	The Spiritual Pandhari	54
XXXII.	"Saints Great of Heart"	55

TUKĀRĀM

XXXIII.	The Mother's House	56
XXXIV.	The Suppliant	56
XXXV.	A Beggar for Love	57
XXXVI.	"God Who is Our Home"	57
XXXVII.	The Strife of Sense	58
XXXVIII.	Waiting	58
XXXIX.	Desolation	59
XL.	"Thee, Lord of Pity, I Beseech" ..	60
XLI.	From the Depths	61
XLII.	Forsake Me Not!	61
XLIII.	Mother Vithoba	62
XLIV.	Me Miserable	62
XLV.	Within My Heart	62
XLVI.	The Restless Heart	63
XLVII.	"I Long to See Thy Face"	64
XLVIII.	"Keep Me from Vanity"	64
XLIX.	Aspiration	64
L.	The Only Refuge	65
LI.	Desolate	65
LII.	"O Save Me, Save Me!"	66
LIII.	Near Yet Far	66
LIV.	Beyond the Mountains, God	67
LV.	"I Cannot Understand: I Love" ..	67
LVI.	Not One But Two	68
LVII.	Man's Extremity	68
LVIII.	Though He Slay Me	69
LIX.	Pandurang	70
LX.	Complete Surrender	70
LXI.	To Thy Dear Feet!	70

		PAGE
LXII.	He Leadeth Me	71
LXIII.	The Joy of the Name	71
LXIV	Love's Captive	72
LXV.	The Bhakta's Duty	72
LXVI.	Love Finds Out God	73
LXVII.	"God is Ours"	73
LXVIII.	"One Thing I Do	74
LXIX.	He Knows Our Needs	74
LXX.	"In Him Abide"	75
LXXI.	The Boldness of Faith	75
LXXII.	Beata Culpa	75
LXXIII.	The Snare of Pride	76
LXXIV.	I Am Poor and Needy	76
LXXV.	A Blind Leader of the Blind	76
LXXVI.	The Pride of Knowledge	77
LXXVII.	The Unveiling of Love	77
LXXVIII.	The Haven	78
LXXIX.	Weariness	78
LXXX.	God's Counterfeit	79
LXXXI.	Self-Surrender	79
LXXXII.	Dying to Live	79
LXXXIII.	The Root of Longing	80
LXXXIV.	The Secret of Peace	80
LXXXV.	The Fellowship of Saints	81
LXXXVI.	The Simple Path	81
LXXXVII.	The Way of Love	81
LXXXVIII.	The Thief	82
LXXXIX.	The Traveller	82
XC.	By Faith Alone	83
XCI.	A Steadfast Mind	83
XCII.	The Name of the Living One	83
XCIII.	The Dedicated Life	84
XCIV.	The Inward Purpose	85
XCV.	The Bhakta's Task	85
XCVI.	Maya	85
XCVII.	"The World Passeth Away"	86
XCVIII.	The Way of Death	86
XCIX.	"The Night Cometh"	87
C.	'Tis All for Naught	87

		PAGE
CI.	The Divine Inspiration	88
CII.	Drowning Men	88
CIII.	Without and Within	88
CIV.	"And Have Not Charity"	89
CV.	The Mendicant	89
CVI.	The Proud Advaitist	89
CVII.	The Hypocrite: I	90
CVIII.	The Hypocrite: II	90
	Bibliography	91
	Index I	93
	Index II	95

INTRODUCTION

THE period of the Marāṭhā renaissance, during which the great poets and saints of Mahārāṣṭra flourished, extends from the thirteenth to the seventeenth century. This literary revival found its impulse in a religious awakening. It is indeed appropriate to call the poets of this period psalmists, because their most characteristic, certainly their most popular, work consisted of short lyrical utterances, called *abhaṅgs*, which usually express religious longing or describe religious experience. All those whose work is represented in this volume were Vaiṣṇavites, adherents of the *bhakti* sect, whose members, while they are to be found at many different periods and in many different districts of India, and while they worshipped a variety of deities, are united in seeking to reach God by the path of *bhakti*, or loving devotion. Most of these saints were at the same time, according to the tradition, ardent devotees of Viṭhobā of Paṇḍharpūr. How the shrine of this god became the high place of *bhakti* worship in the Marāṭhā country we cannot now tell. It is sufficient to say that around it and its god, Viṭhobā or Viṭṭhal, whose name is believed by some scholars to be a corruption of Viṣṇu and who is identified with Kṛiṣṇa, has gathered for many centuries the devotion of a great company of worshippers, who come there on pilgrimage singing songs of praise. Those saints who in their lives centuries ago had been devoted to the god are still borne in palankins, in which are placed models of their holy footprints, to the presence of Viṭhobā in this village on the river Bhimā.

> On Bhimā's banks all gladness is
> In Paṇḍharī, abode of bliss.

This is the refrain of many a song that is re-echoed by the choirs of singers that journey with eager expectation year by year, to this Deccan village to look upon the face of the god.

There is little outwardly to distinguish the worship at this shrine from that of a hundred others throughout the land. The image is rudely fashioned and has no grace of form.[1] The worship is that which is commonly performed in any Hindu temple. What gives it its distinctive character is the special song-services, the *kīrtans* and *bhajans* that are conducted for the instruction of pilgrims, and in which their deep religious emotion finds its fullest utterance. Great numbers of pilgrims sit for hours at Paṇḍharpūr and the other village centres of the cult, listening to the exhortations of some famous preacher or *Haridās*, who bases his discourse upon verses from such poet-saints as Jñāndev or Ekanāth or Tukārām. With the teaching is skilfully combined the singing of a choir. These *kīrtans* have a profound emotional effect upon the multitudes gathered in eager expectation at the holy place. The songs of the old saints awaken, and in some degree satisfy, the deep desires of their hearts. So also groups will gather for what are called *bhajans*, when there is no preaching but they continue often for hours singing those songs of longing and of ecstacy.

It would be easy to show that this religious and intellectual awakening was part of a movement widely spread throughout India. It is, however, only with the Marāṭhā poet saints that we are here concerned. In its influence upon all strata of society this movement, in the opinion of Mr. M. G. Ranade, was far more powerful than the corresponding movement in northern and eastern India. Certainly its leaders were drawn from every class, from the highest to the humblest. "Roughly speaking," says Mr. Ranade in his *Rise of the Marāṭhā Power*, "we may state that the history of the religious revival in Maharāṣṭra covers a period of nearly five hundred years, and during this period some fifty saints and prophets flourished in this land who left their mark upon the country and its people. A few of these saints were women, a few were Muḥam-

[1] See frontispiece.

madan converts to Hinduism, nearly half of them were Brāhmans, while there were representatives in the other half from among all the other castes, Marāṭhās, *kunbīs*, tailors, gardeners, potters, goldsmiths, repentant prostitutes, and slave girls, even the out-caste Mahārs." From the traditional account of some of these saints, as well as from a study of their voluminous poems, we can form some conception of the character of this remarkable movement.

The earliest of them all, a dimly discerned but powerful figure, is a Brāhman, named Jñāneśvar, whose chief work, the *Jñāneśvarī*, can be dated with certainty, having been completed in the year A.D. 1290. "Jñāneśvar's influence," says Mr. Ranade, "has been greater than that of any other Marāṭhā *sādhu* (saint) except Tukārām. . . . Jñāneśvar appeals to the pantheistic tendencies of our people's intellect, while the charm of Tukārām and Nāmdev lies in their appeal to the heart and in the subjective truth of the experiences felt by them in common with all who are religious by nature." To the common people the author of the *Jñāneśvarī* is little more than the shadow of a great name, but it is a name that is linked with that of Tukārām in the songs that they sing as they go on pilgrimage to the shrine at Paṇḍharpūr. As they go they chant two names in chorus, as the names of the chief prophets of their faith, "Jñānobā, Tukārām; Jñānobā, Tukārām." These two, the one in the thirteenth and the other in the seventeenth century, may, with Nāmdev, whom we may place between them in the fourteenth century, be taken as representative in their life and in their influence of the whole of this social and religious quickening in the Marāṭhā country. From the traditional accounts of these saints—even though these are largely legendary and unreliable—as well as from the specimens of their voluminous poems that are translated here, we may be able to form some conception of the character of this remarkable movement.

The life of Jñāneśvar is surrounded by many obscurities. Much controversy has centred round the question whether there were not really two Jñāneśvars, the one the author of the *Jñāneśvarī* and the *Amṛit Anubhāv*—both of them poems of a philosophical or theological character—the other the author of *abhaṅgs* or short lyrics, the utterances of a much more popular and personal religion. The question is one which cannot be investigated here, but it must be admitted that the hypothesis that there were really two of the name resolves some difficulties which the traditional history undoubtedly presents. If, however, we accept the traditional account, this Brāhman poet belonged to Ālandī, a village twelve miles north of Poona. His father had come there when on pilgrimage and had married a woman of the place, but, presently, he resumed his wandering, and proceeded to Benares. He spent some time there under the instruction of a *guru*, or spiritual teacher, but presently the *sannyāsī*, in defiance of religious law and usage, resumed his family duties and returned to Ālandī. Three sons and a daughter were born to him, but when this grave irregularity of conduct was known he was excommunicated. The persecution that he and his wife had to endure is said to have caused them to commit suicide, but their inheritance of trouble passed to the children, who suffered much at the hands of the Brāhmans.

Jñāneśvar's two brothers, Nivṛittināth, who was the eldest of the family, and Sopāndev, and his sister, Muktābāī, are all said to have been, like himself, saints and poets. Some of the legendary tales that have been handed down furnish indications of the conflict with Brāhmanical authority and orthodoxy, which evidently centred around these "*sannyāsī's* children." Jñāneśvar is said to have confounded his Brāhman persecutors by causing a buffalo to recite the Vedas, though these are scriptures that only the twice-born may read. He is alleged, on another occasion, to have gone riding on a wall to meet a famous Brāhman *yogī* and miracle-worker, who, to impress young heretics, was approaching him riding on a tiger with a snake for a whip.

The work upon which Jñāneśvar's fame chiefly rests is the *Jñāneśvarī*, a free and copious paraphrase in Marāṭhī verse of the *Bhagavadgītā*. The seven hundred *ślokas* of the *Gītā* are here expanded into ten thousand verses. This poem forms, perhaps, the most important work in all Marāṭhī literature, and has exercised a unique influence both upon the thought and upon the language of Mahārāṣṭra. The fact that Jñāneśvar used the people's language to convey thoughts hitherto concealed in Sanskrit and so reserved for the learned, was in itself an indication that a new religious spirit was abroad. What he did for Marāṭhī has been compared to what Dante did for Italian. He loved the "national Marāṭhī speech," and showed how it could convey sweet sounds and "clear thoughts like moonlight," and how in his verse "lotus flowers spring up in such abundance." "All the weight and distinction that the Marāṭhī language possesses," says Mr. M. G. Ranade, "it owes to Jñāneśvar. . . . To realize the depth of meaning that is contained in the language one must study the *Jñāneśvarī*."

The tradition affirms that Jñāneśvar, like most of the Marāṭhī school of *bhakti*, was a devotee of Viṭhobā of Paṇḍharpūr. It is strange, therefore, to find no mention of this god in either the *Jñāneśvarī*, or his other philosophical poem, the *Amṛit Anubhāv*. Perhaps it may have been another and later poet of the same name who is the author of these shorter songs or psalms, and who is linked in the legend with the next notable saint of the succession. This is Nāmdev, the author of many simple and passionate lyrics that give expression to varying phases of an ardent devotion to the god of Paṇḍharpūr. The language of Nāmdev's verses is much more modern than that of the *Jñāneśvarī*, so that, though the tradition gives his date as from 1270 to 1350, the probabilities are that Sir R. G. Bhandarkar is right in placing him a century later. He was born in a village near Karhād, in the Sātāra District. How it came about that Nāmdev's heart turned with such passionate adoration to Viṭhobā is somewhat obscure. According to one account he bore, like many other saints, from his infancy the marks of sainthood. The first word he spoke was "Śrī Viṭṭhal"; he learned nothing at school, for he cared for nothing but *kīrtans* (services of song). That is one way in which saints are made, but another is the way of conversion, and there seems to be more authority for the story that Nāmdev was converted from an evil life to service of Viṭhobā.[1] Several *abhangs*—among others one said to be by his wife—refer to an early career of lawlessness brought to a sudden end by his contrition at the tears shed by a woman whom he had made a widow. In his remorse he would have taken his own life in the temple of Nāgnāth, but he found comfort and forgiveness when he sought instead the presence of the more gracious Viṭhobā, and from that day onward he gave himself with complete devotion to the worship of this god.

The chief religious interest in Nāmdev's life lies in tracing a change or development in his thought which his *abhangs* reveal. At first he is the purely emotional *bhakta*, all tears and cries and raptures. Later in his life, however, he seems to have passed through an experience which greatly altered his outlook on the world. In the first stage of his experience Viṭhobā of Paṇḍharī is the sole object of his devotion; he can scarcely tear himself away from the precincts of his temple. At a later period Viṭhobā has become for him no more than a symbol of the supreme soul that pervades the universe. He is still a *bhakta*, but he is no longer visited by the gusts of passion that had once shaken his soul. An attitude of spiritual indifference is now his supreme attainment. His faith rests upon a philosophical interpretation of the universe, which blunts the sensations which formerly harassed him and brings him, if not peace, at least passivity. This change, or growth, is reflected in his *abhangs*, which have not, of course, come down to us in their historical setting or in the order of their composition.

One of the members of Nāmdev's household has also a place among the Marāṭhā poet saints. This is a Śudra woman, named Janabāī, who, according to the story, became a domestic slave of the poet because of her admiration of his devotion. She spent her whole life in his service and Viṭhobā's. The god is declared in the legend to have been

[1] There is curious confirmation of this in the recently discovered and very early book *Līlā Caritra*, a scripture of the interesting sect of Mānbhāūs

constantly in her company, grinding corn for her, drawing water, helping her to wash the clothes. It is not always clear, however, whether the *abhaṅgs* do not really describe, not a personal relationship of communion, but a recognition of the divine immanence in all things. When she says that, "in the inner shrine of contemplation Pāṇḍuraṅg comes to meet us and clasps us to his breast," it is difficult to believe that she is not describing an experience of spiritual fellowship. But when she says, referring to the household occupations,

> Grinding, pounding—this our game,
> Burn we up all sin and shame,

there is here more than a suspicion of *advaita* doctrine. She is reaching beyond the *māyā*, the "sport," of life and its duties to an identity with *Brahman* beyond the distinction of good and evil. This is fully unveiled in another *abhaṅg*,[1] which, after expressing a feeling that has all the appearance of being parallel to that daily comradeship with Christ which Christian saints have ever sought, betrays itself in its conclusion as no more than a metaphysical affirmation of identity with the All.

The new knowledge that he attained and the changed outlook that it brought to him are expressed in his prayer to Viṭhobā: "Let me see thy face with my eyes everywhere and let all creatures be my friends." He has not ceased to follow *bhakti*, but it is no longer with the simplicity of his early love. Far more difficult than to empty the sea or to measure the sky is "the *bhakti* of Keśav," for it requires that all sense of "I" and "thou" shall utterly disappear. "Ah, God, a single atom of distinction is huge as Mount Meru." So also the *bhakta* must realize that God is in all creatures; there must be no love of the flesh, no attachment to the things of sense. He must pass beyond good and evil, beyond love and hate, beyond all storms and tempests into the quiet of passivity. Viṭhobā is now the one real God to him, but not in the sense, as formerly he had thought, that all other gods are false and that he dare not look upon them but only on the idol of Viṭhobā.

[1] No. XXIV, on pp. 49f.

He is the sole-existent *Brahman* with "thousands of worlds in every hair." Nāmdev's denunciations of idolatry in his *abhaṅgs* may be as much inspired by the contempt of the philosopher as by the theistic temper that Muḥammadanism was beginning at this time to introduce to India. Not only, however, does he denounce idolatry and, like Jñāneśvar, the gross, popular worships. He brushes aside, in a fashion that would hardly be possible had he come under the influence of the author of the *Jñāneśvarī*, the authority of the sacred scriptures. "Do not study the Vedas," he says, "needless is scriptural instruction. Repeat the praises of the Name."

Nāmdev obtained *samādhi* at the age of eighty, and is buried at the great door of the temple of Viṭhobā at Paṇḍharpūr. Whoever enters to look upon the face of the god, to whom he rendered such intense devotion, must step across the place where the saint lies buried. Thus he remains still, as it were, a stepping stone to the presence of Viṭhobā.

But of all the Marāṭhā *bhaktas* the greatest in the popular estimation, certainly the widest in the extent of his influence, is Tukārām. He was a contemporary of the Marāṭhā national hero, Śivājī, and it can scarcely be questioned that, by the work that he accomplished in drawing together by means of a common religious enthusiasm all classes of the community, he contributed to the formation under that leader of a Marāṭhā kingdom sufficiently strong and united to resist with success the power of the Mogul Empire. The popularity of his verses has continued undiminished until to-day, and they are so widely known among all classes of Marāṭhās that many of them have almost come to have the vogue and authority of proverbs. They are more familiar throughout Mahārāṣṭra than are (or were) in Scotland "the psalms of David or the songs of Burns." Not only are they prized by the most illiterate worshipper of Viṭhobā as the "Veda" of their sect, but they furnish a large portion of the psalmody of the reforming Prārthanā Samāj, while some of the greatest of modern Indians, such as M. G. Ranade and Sir R. G. Bhandarkar, have found in them, perhaps more than in the ancient scriptures, nourishment for their own religious life.

Tukārām was a Śūdra grain-seller and was born in 1608 at Dehū, a village about eighteen miles north-west of Poona. He had an inherited interest in the god, Viṭhobā, for his family for at least seven generations had been devout worshippers of the god and had regularly visited his shrine at Paṇḍharpūr. One of his *abhaṅgs* gives an account of the process by which he was drawn from occupation with the world to "lay hold in his heart of the feet of Viṭhobā." It gives us a glimpse of one of those periods of famine that must have been frequent and terrible in these days. It brought him, he says, to poverty and shame and sorrow. One of his two wives perished, and he lets us hear her dying cry, "Food, food." This experience appears to have been what made him give himself with complete devotion to the service of the god. In another *abhaṅg* he tells us how a "king of *gurus*" came to him in a dream, and, giving him the *mantra* or sacred formula, "Rām, Kṛiṣṇa, Hari," pointed him to "the ship of Pāṇḍuraṅg." This mysterious teacher is called Bābājī, and he was of the spiritual line of Rāghav Caitanya and Keśav Caitanya. This may possibly indicate that Tukārām came at some time under the influence of teachers belonging to the Vaiṣṇavite sect founded by Caitanya in Bengal at the beginning of the sixteenth century.

The story of Tukārām shows us a man possessing much unworldly charm of character. His occupation with religion is, indeed, as in the case of Nāmdev, a cause of bitter complaint by his wife. His children can get nothing to eat for their father lives at the temple. There are many tales of his unworldliness, such as how the compassion of the saint—in this respect one of the kin of St. Francis of Assisi—for "his little sisters, the birds," made him allow them to have their will of the grain in the corn fields that he was placed in charge of by the farmer who owned them. Another story tells how the birds, recognizing him as "a friend of all the world," perched fearlessly upon him in the temple court. He does not appear to have gone on pilgrimage, reckoning such religious practices as of no value for the making of men better. Jñāneśvar also had condemned them, but he is said, nevertheless, as we have seen, to have conformed in this matter to the established custom. According to a familiar story, Tukārām refused to travel to Benares, but gave those who were going there and would have him join them an unripe gourd, bidding them dip it in the sacred waters of the Ganges and see if thereby it would become sweet to taste.

Tukārām is said to have suffered much persecution from Brāhmans, who saw in this Śudra's popularity as a religious teacher an infringement of their prerogative. Their opposition is said to have culminated in a command to him to cast his poems into the river Indrāyani, on the bank of which Dehū stands. He obeyed, but his god himself intervened and saved them from destruction. Another story, which appears to be of doubtful authenticity and may have been invented to exalt the poet, represents Śivajī as in vain inviting the humble saint to visit his court, and even, under the spell of Tukārām, as proposing himself to quit his kingdom and give himself up to a life of contemplation. Tukārām is believed to have been miraculously translated to Vaikuṇṭha—the heaven of Viṣṇu—in the year 1649. Several early manuscripts of his poems, however, have simply the statement noted on them that in that year on a certain day he "disappeared," or, according to one of them, "he set out for a holy place."

The most authoritative collection of Tukārām's *abhaṅgs* contains over 4,600 of these poems. This is far short, however, of the number that he is credited with having composed. Nāmdev is said to have enjoined upon him in a dream to produce enough to realize the earlier poet's ambition that the world should possess a hundred *crores* or one billion *abhaṅgs*. As a matter of fact, many even of those that are attributed to him are in all probability forgeries for which popularity and authority have been sought by the help of a great name. This, no doubt, has helped to make still more bewildering the inconsistencies of thought that appear in Tukārām's work, as in all the work of these far from logical or systematic thinkers. Nor are the poems arranged in any chronological order. Any attempt to trace a process of development in the religious ideas they present must accordingly be largely conjectural. As a matter of fact, like so many other Hindu teachers from the days of the *ṛiṣis* of the *Upaniṣads*, Tukārām is claimed by various religious schools—by theists and by pantheistic monists—as an adherent of their views. To explain his inconsistency, however, it is perhaps sufficient to say that he was a poet and that he was a Hindu.

When we turn to consider the character of the teaching of these poet-saints and of the influence that by work so widely popular they exerted and still exert, the first difficulty that presents itself is this inconsistency, which is written upon every page of their work. No doubt the fact that they were Hindus and therefore inheritors in their blood and in the texture of their thought of that Hinduism which is as much a spirit, a temperament, as a system, goes far to explain their mental adjustment to what appear to us irreconcilable explanations of life and destiny. *Advaita* (non-duality) and *bhakti* are not so much, we may say, contradictory theories of the universe as varying moods of the Hindu mind. Certainly *bhakti* in large measure was a mood. It was the other half of *advaita*, a reaction of the soul, a feast of that heart which *advaita* had starved. It is the deliberate choice, after long loneliness, of the companionship of God and the saints; after silence, of song; after bareness and intellectual austerity, of the rich colours of affection. And yet, because it is a reaction and not the result of a reasoned development, it is apt to lapse back to what it has rebelled against. It is not intellectually convinced. It represents a part only of the man and that the part most liable to fluctuations—his emotional life. *Advaita* is equally partial, and hence, perhaps, the oscillations to and fro that mark their thinking. It would be foolish to labour to reduce their teaching to logical consistency. The *bhakta* has his seasons of warmth and exaltation when the supreme bliss is to have fellowship with the god of his devotion and to be conscious of his love, while at other times in colder mood he is content to follow the philosophic path that leads to Nirvāṇa and to nothingness. But the value and significance of this movement lie in its affirmation of the claims of the human heart and in the moral and religious consequences that follow from that affirmation. These are the elements in it that gave it its power and enabled it to make an appeal so far reaching and so profound. It was, if we may say so, a splendid effort of the Hindu soul to break the bondage under which it had lain so long. It at least stirred in its long sleep, and turned its drowsy eyes towards the dawn.

If there was in it this rebel spirit, then there was no tyranny within Hinduism that would so challenge it as the long-established and powerful dominance of caste. A fervent spirit of devotion is inevitably democratic, just as a "way of knowledge" is a way reserved for an intellectual minority while a ceremonial religion strengthens the power and the pride of a priestly order. The heart and its emotions are much the same in all men, high or low, and the road to God along which the affections lead the way is an open road. It is accordingly to be expected that the *bhakti* movement, in so far as it was earnest and sincere, would oppose Brāhman pretentions and caste contempt. We find this to have been in large measure the case. The sect of Caitanya admitted to its ranks even Śūdras and Muḥammadans and they are said to sing of the saint himself in Bengal: "Come see the godman who does not believe in caste." Kabīr is said to have been himself by birth a Muḥammadan who succeeded by strategy in obtaining admission to the number of Rāmānanda's disciples. The Marāṭhā saints were of all castes, from Brāhmans to out-castes. The stories that are told of them, mingled with legend as they are, reveal a continual struggle against injustice. We see it in the story of Jñāneśvar's parents and of the saint's own experience and that of his brothers and sisters. It seems as if Jñāneśvar may have been the centre of a struggle between the old orthodoxy, entrenched within its caste privileges and buttressed by its claims to magic powers, and the new and more living and spiritual faith. We see indications of the same conflict in the case of nearly every one of Jñāneśvar's successors in the *bhakti* line. There is evidence, too, both in the traditions of Nāmdev's life and in his verses, that as a Śūdra he had to face Brāhman contempt, but was sustained by the sympathy of Viṭhobā. Ekanāth, too, who lived at Paithan towards the close of the sixteenth century and was himself a Deśasth Brāhman, continued the struggle and opposed caste both by precept and example. As a consequence he is said to have been out-casted and his poems publicly thrown into the river Godaverī. Tukārām, as we have seen, was punished in the same way, according to the story, and he certainly had to endure much petty persecution because of his denunciation of caste-exclusiveness. Again, another of the saints of Paṇḍharpūr was a member of the out-caste community of Mahārs. This man, Cokā Melā, whose *samādhi* (memorial) is opposite to the entrance to the great temple of Viṭhobā, once, it is said, crossed the threshold of the temple and was cast out for his impiety. He pled in excuse that he had been borne in by a divinely created impulse that he could not resist, and reproached his enemies in pathetic words for their harshness and contempt. On another occasion Viṭhobā himself is said to have helped him to carry off the carcass of a cow, that being one of the perquisites permitted to this out-caste community. These are some indications of what was, we may conjecture, a continuous struggle throughout this whole period between the divisive forces of Brāhman exclusiveness and the sense of kinship and unity that the new religion of faith and fellowship with God inspired.

The message of these poets was opposed to a gross idolatry ; it frequently denounced immorality and superstition ; it was generally sincere and earnest and spiritual. No doubt there are qualifications that have to be added to each of these statements if we are to avoid misunderstanding. Most of these saints were worshippers of the idol, Viṭhobā, but they distinguished between their attitude to this god and that of the superstitious multitude.

A stone with red-lead painted o'er
Brats and women bow before.

When Tukārām says this he implies that he and those like him looked beyond the idol—Viṭhobā, "standing on the brick," as he so often describes him—to something greater that the idol symbolized and signified. So Nāmdev repeatedly denounces idolatry. "No *guru* can show me God: wherever I go there are stone gods painted red. How can a stone god speak? When will he ever utter speech? My mind is weary of those who say, 'God; god.' Everywhere I go they say, 'Worship a stone.' He is God whom Nāma beholds in his heart. Nāma will never forsake the feet of Kṛiṣṇa." They also will make no terms with the impure and degrading worships that they see around them. The evil cult of Khaṇḍobā, the greedy mendicant, the formal and hypocritical priest, the magic worker, all these they deal with in much the same fashion as did Luther and Erasmus with their counterparts in the Christian Church of Europe.

As theists the Marāṭhā psalmists oppose what a South Indian follower of *bhakti* calls "the haughty Vedânt creed." Sometimes they admit that the "way of knowledge" is higher than the way of faith, but that the heart has its reasons, to which they feel they must give heed. Sometimes they go further, and claim their way as the highest. Tukārām in one of his poems describes how those who had chosen the path of *Brahma* knowledge and looked forward to deliverance from re-birth and to final absorption turn back under his guidance to the bondage of life, because with it they can experience a fellowship with God of which they can have conscious experience.[1] He does not wish to be merged in the unconsciousness of *Brahman*, "like the dew drop in the silent sea." This goal, that so fascinates the Brâhman philosopher wearied with the sorrows of existence, has no charm for him. Perhaps this is an indication that life had gained a new interest for the people of that age, with the awakening of some sense of brotherhood among men and some hope that there was love for them in the heart of God. They want to know, as Jñāneśvar says (Jñ. VI, 113), "the bliss of affection."

[1] See No. LXXXVII.

They do not desire even the joys of heaven. Best of all it seems to them to be to remain on earth, in the fellowship of the saints, singing the praises of the god of their devotion. Jñāneśvar in one passage describes such a *bhakta* and his supreme desire. Tukārām is no less emphatic in his rejection of a union that means unconsciousness and an end to the joy of serving and praising his divine Master: "*Advait*," he says, "contents me not."[1]

But in the case of every one of these poets, as we have seen, there is a hesitation and ambiguity when they compare these rival blessednesses. "Knowledge" and *Brahman* have a prestige in India that even Tukārām cannot forget, though he knows by his own experience that knowledge is, as he says, "a stringless lute." It is, in fact, as a Christian *bhakta* had long before declared, "like sounding brass and a clanging cymbal." And yet, Tukārām can hear what Kabīr calls the "unstruck music," and sometimes yields to its subtle fascination. "There," says Kabīr, who has praised the "bliss of affection" with as rapturous a delight as any Marāṭhā saint, "the whole sky is filled with sound, and there that music is made *without fingers and without strings*."[2] In fact, they all want both to have and have not. The unitive life draws them with a desire that so many mystical spirits, East and West alike, have felt. Not in the monism of Śaṅkarācārya, nor in the dualism that is quite satisfied to remain two, but in a spiritual experience that transcends and includes both is peace to be found.

> For only where the one is twain,
> And where the two are one again
> Will truth no more be sought in vain.

Hence the instability, the alternate raptures and despairs of these, as of other, mystic seekers. Love alone—a love that is not a blind rapture but is knowledge too—solves the insoluble problem. "In the contact of the embrace," says Jñāneśvar, "the two become one naturally" (Jñ. V, 133), but they must remain one, not subject to the vacillations of what is a mere sentiment. Sometimes

[1] No. LVI. [2] Tagore's *Hundred Poems of Kabīr*. p. 22.

they persuade themselves that even in the silence of the ultimate unity they will be able to hear what one of them, Kabīr, calls " the music of the forgetting of sorrows."

When one reviews the work of these poets it becomes evident that the scope of the thought and the desires they express is not wide, nor is there a rich variety in their music. It is not quite a symphony " on a penny whistle," but it has much of the simplicity and monotony, as well as of the freshness and sincerity, that George Meredith suggests when he takes that as the symbol of the first love of youth and the springtime. There are no organ notes here, no full volume of harmonious sound. The favourite and most characteristic poetic form made use of by this group of singers is the *abhaṅg*, a brief utterance of usually from ten to thirty lines, a true cry of the heart. The poems of Kabīr and of Sir Rabindranath Tagore appear to be of much the same character. They seem to proceed in most cases from some inward experience and are vivid with emotion. Whether they are cries of longing, or utterances of love and devotion, or endeavours to understand and explain life and destiny, they are never merely decorative in their purpose. They are primarily religious and only secondarily and accidentally works of art. They are psalms—meant to be sung, not said, and inseparable, for a full appreciation, from their music. No doubt the music helps to make up for an occasional poverty of thought and bareness of language, but it enables them also to mount and soar, and carries their message more surely to its lodgment in the hearer's heart. They are thus true lyrics, and their melancholy music makes more touching still the simple appeal in many of them, of which we might almost say that they "have no language but a cry." Their most frequently expressed desire is that they may reach and rest upon the breast of God. They express this longing by means of a rich variety of comparisons, of which the most frequent and most touching is that of a child longing for his mother. It is, perhaps, significant that this relationship is used by the Hebrew saints as a symbol, not of the soul's yearning for God, but of God's yearning over His children. "Can a woman forget her sucking child, that she should not have compassion on the son of her womb? Yea, these may forget, yet will not I forget thee."[1] "As one whom his mother comforteth, so will I comfort you."[2]

It is in these cries of desire that the Marāṭhā singers come nearest to the Hebrew psalmists. It may, perhaps, be maintained with truth that their longing has not the depth and urgency that characterise Hebrew poetry—a depth and urgency that are due to a deeper sense of need. The Hebrew cry is "out of the depths." These Hindu saints frequently express a sense of desolation, of weariness in a world of change and sorrow, of loneliness in separation from God. They say, even as the Hebrew does, "Like as the hart panteth for the water-brooks, so panteth my soul after thee, O God,"[3] but they can scarcely be said to know what he experiences when he goes on to say, "All thy waves and thy billows have gone over me." For the same reason, while there are professions of fervent devotion and affection, while occasional experiences of inward bliss in the divine fellowship are described, there is not the deep note of gratitude which is often sounded in the music of Hebrew psalmists. They knew little of such an experience as that which is described in the words, "He brought me up out of an horrible pit, out of the miry clay; and he set my feet upon a rock and established my goings. And he hath put a new song in my mouth."[4] The resonant note of thankfulness which throbs in the 103rd Psalm is outside of their knowledge. They can venture, on the contrary, to say of these who love God, "God is *their* debtor now."[5] Such an audacity is beyond the reach of the Hebrew or the Christian penitent, unless his conscience of sin and of unworthiness is overlaid with pantheistic speculation as was that of the mediæval mystic, Eckhart, who says of God, "He can as little do without me as I can do without Him."

It is, perhaps, on the whole true to say that the Hindu psalmists give expression to a more purely natural affection,

[1] Isaiah, XLIX, 15. [2] Isaiah, LXVI, 12. [3] Ps. XLII, 1. [4] Ps. XL, 2, 3. [5] No. LXXXVII, p. 81.

one less suffused with moral meaning, than that which we find in the Hebrew psalms. They feel in fellowship with God the instinctive satisfaction, as they so often describe it, that a babe feels on his mother's breast. Nearness to God is simply their proper element, as water is to a fish. If it is the case that the sense of sin is a morbid growth in man's experience, if there is no ground in the truth of things to justify the feeling of separation on the part of a sinful man from a holy God and the demand for a mediator, then these Indian saints have found a nearer and a directer way to God than the Hebrew and Christian penitents. But, on the other hand, no one can question the claim that the Hebrews, and far more, of course, the Christians, have from the dark places of their experience described a more gracious and tender aspect of God and are far more sure of His love. The god the Hindu aspires towards is capricious in his affection; the relation of love between him and his worshipper is not based on a strong assurance of his unwavering righteousness. This marks a profound difference of tone between the religious experience of the saints of India and of Judea, a difference which really denotes the distinction that formerly was made between natural and revealed religion. There is a strength, a depth, an assurance in the one—in spite of many tremors—that is not in the other. The beauty, the pathos, the charm of Hindu piety, as here expressed, consists in the very earthliness and uncertainty of its eager hopes. Hebrew aspiration has its roots in darker depths, but it is met by a revelation—an assurance, that is, that comes to the desiring heart—of God's moral majesty as well as of His grace, which gives it quietness and confidence and strength. This assurance—which rises to rapture and triumph in the New Testament—is already present in the psalmists and prophets of the Old Testament with a richness far beyond anything within the compass of the music of these Indian singers. At the same time it would be untrue to say that there are not a certain number of expressions of content and of satisfied affection in their songs, or that they have no experience of peace in the divine fellowship. Examples of such joy and satisfaction are to be found especially among the psalms of Tukārām.[1]

There are other respects, in addition to those which have been noted, in which the deep division between the Hindu and Hebrew psalmists reveals itself, hidden as it is beneath the common need of hearts that are at one in their longing to find rest in God. As the one conceives of God as being beyond everything else a moral Being, while to the other He is still not much more than a pervading presence in nature, without clearly defined moral characteristics, their ideals of the holy life are fundamentally divergent. "Who shall ascend into the hill of the Lord?" says the Hebrew, "Or who shall stand in his holy place? He that hath clean hands and a pure heart; who hath not lifted up his soul unto vanity nor sworn deceitfully. He that walketh uprightly and worketh righteousness and speaketh truth in his heart. . . . In whose eyes a vile person is condemned; but he honoureth them that fear the Lord. He that sweareth to his hurt and changeth not. He that putteth not out his money to usury, nor taketh reward against the innocent. He that doeth these things shall never be moved."[2] Such passages as these describe an attitude of practical philanthropy; they recognise the supremacy of moral demands and the claims of duty to one's neighbour. The religion of the Hebrew psalmists is, no doubt, predominantly personal and individual, but the needs of others and responsibility for others are never far from the worshipper's thoughts. God is for him the God not merely of the individual worshipper but of at least the nation. He is also often recognised as the King over the whole earth, the Judge who will judge the world with righteousness and the people with equity. These things belong to a conception of God and of His relations with men completely different from that of the Indian devotees. For them the ideal man is one who has reached a haven of tranquillity.

> No wind of good or ill
> Shall enter there,

[1] See Nos. LXII, LXIII and LXXXII. [2] Ps. XV.

> But peace, supremely still,
> Supremely fair.[1]

Equanimity is his supreme quality. He looks with an equal mind upon "a very courteous Brāhman, a dog or an out-caste man" (Bhagavadgītā, v. 18). His compassion is measured and controlled, and strong feeling never agitates his soul. In Tukārām's description of the man who is "God's own counterfeit"[2] we have the Indian ideal at its very best, one conscious of duty to others but not urgently or passionately moved to discharge it, more concerned with the cultivation of a placid temper in himself than with the wrongs and sorrows of other men. There is much that is singularly attractive in this picture, especially to those who suffer from the fever and the fret of modern Western life. As described by one who was deeply distressed by the futile agitations of our pursuits, we

> Glance and nod and bustle by,
> And never once possess our souls
> Before we die.

The surge of all anger and passion is to be by the Indian saint most anxiously avoided.

> Thou pervading Brahman art,
> How should anger fill thy heart ?[3]

"Calm *is* life's crown," says Tukārām, contradicting by anticipation Matthew Arnold.

It follows inevitably from this difference in the ideal of the holy life and in the conception of the character of God that the Indian saints have no vision of a world judged or a world redeemed. Their horizon is very narrow and limited, and their god is their own personal god—not the nation's or the world's. He is with them most often as a mother with her child or as a bridegroom with the bride —never as a King ruling a people in righteousness, or as a Judge, "the Most High over all the earth." The choice for the Hindu religion seems to lie between a provincial or village deity, on the one hand, and a *Brahman*, on the other, whose rule, if it can be called rule, may extend more

[1] No. LXXVIII. [2] No. LXXX, p. 79. [3] No. X.

widely, but extends over an empty and silent land, a "wide, grey, lampless, deep, unpeopled world."

One most noticeable difference between the Indian and the Hebrew psalmists is that the former betray scarcely a trace of the fierce, Hebrew passion of revenge, of the spirit of vindictiveness, the cry for vengeance, that deforms so many of the Biblical psalms. There is nothing in this Indian sacred poetry to correspond to the prayer, "Pour out thy wrath upon the heathen that have not known thee, and upon the kingdoms that have not called upon thy name." Though about the time when these worshippers of Viṭhobâ sang their songs the Muḥammadans were invading the land, breaking in pieces their gods and committing, we may be sure, many a crime, there is no cry to God in these poems for vengeance upon them. Nāmdev refers to these things, but with no anger: he has reached a region of indifference to such matters. "A god of stone," he says contemptuously, "and a worshipper who is deceived. . . . Such gods were broken in pieces by the Turks. They threw them into the river, as all men know." No doubt they would say to the Muḥammadan marauder, as a "holy man" is said to have said to a British soldier who stabbed him in the days of the Mutiny, "And thou, too, art He." All feelings are diluted and all differences, even the difference of right and wrong, are harmonised in a world pervaded by an impersonal, unmoral spirit, likeness to whom—or which—is the highest attainment. This doctrine, we must remember, is behind even the theism of these saints, emptying their hearts of strong passions,—whether the desire for vengeance or the desire for justice, whether the desire to punish evil-doers or to save the perishing. Occasionally Tukārām's heart,—for it certainly is a very tender heart,—feels and recognises the claim that human need makes upon him—

> Can my heart unmovèd be,
> When before my eyes I see
> Drowning men ?—[1]

[1] No. CII.

but this is a rare mood and very seldom expressed in his poems. His own need and his own concerns absorb him, and it is not his business to call down vengeance upon evil doers or to right the world's injustices.

What, then, is the essential difference between the religious contribution of the Hebrew and of the Hindu psalmists? The answer is not to be found in the greater intensity of the desire for God or the subtler intellectual insight of the one group of saints or of the other. It is something that reaches deeper in what is beyond all else a moral universe. The Hebrew saints and prophets realised earlier and with a profounder grasp than any other people that it is only the pure in heart that can truly see God, that it is in "mortal, moral strife" that He is alone aright revealed. The way of moral progress, of the purging of the eye of the soul that can see God, is not the way of the conscience dulled and deadened and of the heart emptied of feeling. On the contrary, it is by reinforcing the power in man to love righteousness and hate iniquity and by drawing his heart towards holiness that he is brought into any real divine fellowship. The conscience of the Hebrew psalmist is far from being fully enlightened: his personal enemies are often reckoned as God's enemies and his private vendetta given a divine sanction. But the Jew is more deeply right than any other people in building everything ultimate in his universe upon the distinction between right and wrong. "There is nothing in the world or out of it that is good except a good will." The Hebrew saints built all their dreams and hopes of God and of the eternal world of "stuff o' the conscience," and for that reason they built what has endured.

The saints of *bhakti* not infrequently indeed make moral affirmations that prove them to have had visions of this highway to the presence of God. Especially is this true of Tukārām. One couplet of his has acquired the familiarity of a proverb among Marāṭhās, and must have taught them many a lesson of sincerity and straightforwardness.

He whose words and acts agree,
Let his footsteps praisèd be.

Still more striking is another passage in which he describes the heart to which God makes Himself known: "Pity, patience, calm—that is God's dwelling-place." There is, no doubt, more breadth and exaltation, as well as a profounder sense of human sin and the alienation that it brings, in the Hebrew prophet's declaration, "Thus saith the high and lofty One that inhabiteth eternity, whose name is Holy. I dwell in the high and holy place, with him also who is of a contrite and humble spirit, to revive the spirit of the humble and to revive the heart of the contrite one."[1] For he knows, as Tukārām scarcely does, that "the sacrifices of God are a broken heart." It is the tears of penitence, through whose veil alone a sinful man discerns the face of God.

[1] Isaiah LVII, 15.

NOTE

The titles of the selections are in all cases due to the translator. Selections I-IV, XXVI and XXVIII are portions extracted from long expository or narrative poems, the names of which are given in the notes. All the other selections are short lyrical poems, called *abhangs*, bearing no title but usually referred to by their opening words. There are various kinds of *abhangs*, some having two lines to a verse, some four. One of the commonest rhymes and divides its verse somewhat as is done in No. XCVI. Another very simple form is almost exactly reproduced in translation No. XLIV. The six selections mentioned above, which are not *abhangs*, are in the *ovī* metre, which has usually a triple rhyme. This has been followed in the translations.

The last verse of an *abhang* opens usually with the name of the author—"Tukā says," or "Nāma says," or some similar phrase. This has frequently been followed in the translations, but not always.

For purposes of reference the opening words of each *abhang* are given under the title, the words being transliterated from the Marāṭhī in accordance with the scheme of transliteration shown below. At the same time a reference is given in the case of the *abhangs* of Nāmdev and of one or two others to Avate's edition of these poets, and in the case of Tukārām to the *Indu Prakash* edition of his works published in Bombay (referred to as I.P.).

SYSTEM OF TRANSLITERATION

अ a, आ ā, इ i, ई ī, उ u, ऊ ū, ऋ ṛ, ए e, ऐ ai, ओ o, औ au, क k, ख kh, ग g, घ gh, ङ ṅ; च c, छ ch, ज j, झ jh, ञ ñ; ट ṭ, ठ ṭh, ड ḍ, ढ ḍh, ण ṇ; त t, थ th, द d, ध dh, न n; प p, फ ph, ब b, भ bh, म m; य y, र r, ल l, व v, श ś, ष ṣ, स s, ह h, ळ ḷ; *visarga* ḥ, nasalised म् as in संयम ṁ.

JNĀNEŚVAR[1]

(13th Century)

I. THE GREAT HEARTED

(Jñāneśvarī IX, 188ff.)

Who day and night are from all passion free,—
Within their holy hearts I love to be,
Dwelling in sanctity.

Hearts of a fervent faith to them belong,
Where Dharma[2] reigns; in them that power is strong
That knows or right or wrong.

They bathe in Wisdom; then their hunger stay
With Perfectness; lo, all in green array,
The leaves of Peace are they.

Buds of Attainment these; columns they are
In Valour's hall: of joy fetched from afar
Each a full water-jar.

So dear the path of *bhakti*, they despise
The great Release;[3] e'en in their sport there lies
The Wisdom of the wise.

With pearls of Peace their limbs they beautify;
Within their minds as in a scabbard I,
The All-indweller,[4] lie.

Therefore their love waxes unceasingly,—
These greatsouled ones; not the least rift can be
Between their hearts and me.

[1] For some account of this poet and the poem from which selections I-IV are taken, see pp. 13ff.

[2] *Dharma*, the whole body of moral and religious law by which the social structure, connoted by the term *caste*, is maintained in Hinduism.

[3] *The Great Release*, *mukti*, or *mokṣa*, that is, absorption in the Supreme Spirit, which brings deliverance from rebirth. The saint who follows *bhakti* prefers to live on earth, in the fellowship of the saints, singing the praises of his God. Cf. Nos. LXXXVII, XCII.

[4] *The All-indweller*, that is, Kṛiṣṇa, who is the speaker.

II. THE RAPTURE OF DEVOTION

(*Jñāneśvarī IX, 197ff.*)

Dancing they sing my praises ;[1] surely not
For them rites of atonement,—nay, I wot,
Sin's very name's forgot.

The mind and heart ask, "What shall we restrain ?"
The sacred stream cries, "All my cleansing's vain,
Since here there is no stain."

Thus by the praises of my name they slay
The world's distress ; hark, how it echoes gay
With happy holiday.

The same to them the monarch or his thrall,
The high or low,—themselves alike to all
A place of festival.

To heaven they seldom go,[2] but earth they fill
Brim full of heaven, chanting my name until
The world is cleansed from ill.

For not in heaven I dwell ; nor in the sky
In the sun's orb ; than *yogī's*[3] visions high
Far higher still am I.

Not in such places, Pāṇḍav,[4] I abide,
But those who sing my praises far and wide,
Within their hearts I hide.

How glad of heart are they beholding me.
Forgot are time and place ; where'er they be,
There sing they joyfully.

And they, the while my name they celebrate
In endless song, with limpid thought debate
Upon the soul's estate.

[1] *My praises.* Kṛiṣṇa is the speaker.
[2] *To heaven they seldom go.* Compare Note 3 on p. 35.
[3] *Yogī*, one who seeks absorption in the Supreme Spirit by mental exercises and concentration.
[4] *Pāṇḍav*, that is, Arjuṇa, to whom Kṛiṣṇa is speaking.

III. AEQUANIMITAS

(*Jñāneśvarī XII, 197ff.*)

His heart, O Arjuṇa, no bias knows:
On all an equal aspect he bestows,
Friends let them be or foes.

A lamp is he, shining with steadfast light,
Not shining to the stranger dark as night,
While to the household bright.

As trees whose shadows on their planter fall
Or on who hews them down,—so he to all
Alike impartial.

Sweet to its tender is the cane; nor less
To him who crushed it in the cruel press,—
Sweet with no bitterness;

So he who deems a friend or foe the same,
Alike unmovèd though the world should blame,
Or though it grant him fame.

Lo, as the unperturbèd skies enfold
The changing seasons, does this one behold
Or scorching heat or cold.

Whether a north wind or a south wind blow
It matters not to Meru,[1]—even so
To him is joy or woe.

Ah, sweetly, sweetly does the moonlight fall
Alike upon the monarch and the thrall,—
So he the same to all.

IV. TRUTH.

(*Jñāneśvarī XVI, 115ff.*)

How tender is the bud, yet mark aright
How sharp it thrusts; and how the moon is bright
Though gently falls its light.

[1] *Meru*, the central mountain of the universe, round which the planets revolve.

Or of what medicine can any tell
But bitter is, that makes the sick man well?
(Dost mark my parallel?)

Soft as the water 'tis, that gives no pain
E'en to the eyeball, but that sweeps amain
And rends the earth in twain.

To pierce our doubts it's sharper than a spear,—
And yet than sweetness self how much more dear
To the attentive ear.

The ear receives it with a deep delight,
And on it travels till by truth's own might
It climbs to Brahma's height.[1]

Ah, who by love of truth was e'er deceived?
Or who, when truth he rightly has received,
Has e'er by her been grieved?

V. "CRY HARI"[2]

(Devāciye dvārī ubhā kṣaṇabharī)

Stand at the door of God
One moment nigh,—
Thou hast the fourfold bliss
Obtained thereby.

Cry "Hari," cry aloud,—
Let the name ring;
So thou shalt merit gain
Past reckoning.

Dwell in the world, but still
Cry out amain,—
Witness the ancient saints,—
Thou shalt attain.

[1] *Brahma's height*, the final goal of Hinduism is the realisation of identity with Brahma.

[2] *Hari*, one of the names of Viṣṇu or Kṛiṣṇa, popularly interpreted to mean "the remover of sin."

Yea (hark to Jñānadev[1])
Vyāsa[2] has told
How to the Pāṇḍavs' house
God came of old.

VI. THE NAME

(*Santāce saṅgatī manomārgagatī*)

To the dwelling of the saints
Take thy way;
There the Lord himself shall not
Say thee nay.

Cry "Rāmkṛiṣṇa",—'tis the path
To life's goal.
Worship Rāma,—he who is
Śiva's soul.

Him whose name is unity,
Whoso find,
Fetters of duality
Cannot bind.

All the lustre and the glow
Yogīs[3] gain
By this name so honey-sweet
We attain.

On Pralhāda's[4] childish lips
Dwelt the name,
While to Uddav bringing gifts
Kṛiṣṇa came.

Easy 'tis to utter it
(Is't not true?)
Yet who use it anywhere
Ah, how few.

[1] *Jñānadev*, a variant of the author's name, Jñāneśvar.
[2] *Vyāsa*, the traditional author of the great epic, the Mahābhārata, the theme of which is the fortunes of five brothers, the Pāṇḍavas.
[3] *Yogīs*, see above, p. 36.
[4] *Pralhāda* and *Uddhav*, famous Vaiṣṇava devotees of ancient legend.

VII. "THERE NEEDS NOT AN APPOINTED HOUR'

(*Kāḷaveḷa nāma uccāritā nāhī*)

There needs not a propitious hour
    This name to cry.
Lo, both who speaks it and who hears
    Are saved thereby.

This holy name bears quite away
    All man's offence,—
Hari, the saviour e'en of men
    Of little sense.

Who speak this name, the soul of all,
    O happy they!
Plain for their fathers' feet they make
    The heavenward way.

VIII. THE STOREHOUSE OF BLISS

(*Rūpa pāhātā locanī*)

When thy visage I descry,
O how glad, how glad am I!

Viṭṭhal[2] 'tis, the good the fair,—
Mādhav, good beyond compare.

Many blessings gather here,—
How can Viṭṭhal but be dear?

Every joy is found in thee,
Father, Lord of Rukminī.

[1] This is the first *abhang* sung in every *bhajan*. See p. 12.
[2] *Viṭṭhal*, one of the names of Viṭhobā, the form of Kṛiṣṇa, worshipped at Paṇḍharpūr. Mādhav is another name of Kṛiṣṇa, whose wife is Rukminī.

MUKTĀBĀĪ

(13th Century)

IX. THE LAND OF TOPSY-TURVY[1]

(*Muṅgī uḍālī ākāśī*)

An ant has leapt up to the sky
And swallowed up the sun on high!

A marvel this that I declare,—
That barren wife a son should bear.

A scorpion plumbs the nether Pit,
And Viṣṇu's snake bows down to it.

A fly an eagle brings to birth.
Muktā, beholding, laughs with mirth.

X. A REMONSTRANCE[2]

(*Majavarī dayā karā*)

Graciously thy heart incline:—
Open to me, brother mine!

He's a saint who knoweth how
To the world's abuse to bow.

Great of soul indeed is he,—
Wholly purged of vanity.

Surely he whose soul is great
Is to all compassionate.

Thou pervading Brahman art.
How should anger fill thy heart?

Such a poisèd soul be thine.
Open to me, brother mine!

[1] This Land of Topsy-turvy is the land of the enlightened soul, where all is One.

[2] This *Abhaṅg* is said to have been addressed by Muktābāī to her brother Jñānvéṣvar on an occasion when the door of his hut was closed against her and she supposed him to be angry.

NĀMDEV

(14th Century)

XI. "GONE ARE THE SAINTS"

(*Āvaṭe, 938. Gele digambara īśvaravibhūti*)

Gone are the saints, passed to the heavenly sphere ;
Only their fame tarries behind them here.

Our ears have heard of their unworldly ways,—
But there are no saints like them nowadays.

Men talk of knowledge,—say, "It's this and this,"
But still Nivṛitti's[1] way to truth they miss.

They'll show us Parabrahm,[2] they say ; but, ah,
There's no one has the skill of Jñānobā.

They talk of bliss of earth and bliss divine,
But only Sopāndev can say, "'Tis mine."

Ah, God, says Nāmdev, say we what we will,
Thy secret, Muktābāī, escapes us still.

XII. THE HEART'S DESIRE

(*Kitī, devā, tuhma yēu kākuḷatī*)

O God, my cry comes up to thee,—
  How sad a cry is it !
What is this tragic destiny
  That fate for me has writ ?

[1] On Nivṛitti, Sopāndev and Muktābāī, see p. 14.

[2] *Parabrahm*, the supreme *Brahman*.

Wherefore, O Hṛiṣīkeś,[1] dost thou
So lightly pass me by?
To whom, to whom but to thee now
Can I lift up my cry?

As chiming anklets sweetly ring
So rings thy name abroad;
To human spirits hungering
Thou givest peace with God.

Thou on thy shoulders carrying
All the world's load of care,—
To thee 'tis such a little thing
My trouble too to bear!

O Mother Pāṇḍuraṅg,[2] I cry,
Drive thou me not away.
At Hari's feet I, Nāma, lie;
He will not say me nay.

XIII. "O HASTE AND COME"

(*Āvaṭe, 1482. Kāya mājhā ātā pāhātosi anta*)

Dost thou behold me perishing?
O haste and come, my God and king.

I die unless thou succour bring,
O haste and come, my God and king.

To help me is a trifling thing;
Yet thou must haste, my God and king.

O come (how Nāma's clamours ring)
O haste and come, my God and king.

[1] *Hṛiṣīkeś*, one of the names of Kṛiṣṇa.

[2] *Pāṇḍuraṅga* is one of the most popular names of Viṭhobā of Paṇdharpūr, and so is equivalent to Kṛiṣṇa or Hari. Here, as in many of the poems that follow, the god is addressed as a mother.

XIV. A VOW

(*Āvaṭe, 333. Deha jāvo athavā rāho*)

Whether I live or perish, yet
On Pāṇḍuraṅg[1] my faith is set.

Thy feet, Lord, I will ne'er forsake,—
To thee this solemn vow I make.

Thy holy name my lips shall tell;
Within my heart thy love shall dwell.

This, Keśav,[1] is thy Nāma's vow.
O aid me to fulfil it, thou!

XV. ONE THING

(*Āvaṭe, 501. Heci devā pai māgata*)

One thing I of my Lord entreat,
That I may ever serve his feet.

That I in Paṇḍharī[2] abide,
Always his holy saints beside.

Or high or low my birth may be;
Still, Hari, I would worship thee!

Lord of Kamalā,[3] Nāma prays,
O grant me this through all my days.

XVI. A BITTER CRY

(*Āvaṭe, 351. Mājhī koṇa gatī sāṅgā*)

When will the end of these things be?
Ah, tell me, Lord of Paṇḍharī.[4]
When wilt thou save unhappy me?

O tell me, tell me true, for I
Cry to thee with a bitter cry.

[1] *Pāṇḍuraṅg* and *Keśav*, names of Kṛiṣṇa or Viṭhobā.
[2] *Paṇḍharī*, Paṇdharpūr, see p. 11.
[3] *Lord of Kamalā*, Viṣṇu or Kṛiṣṇa, Kamalā being a name of Lakṣmī, his wife.
[4] *Lord of Paṇḍharī*, Viṭhobā. See p. 11.

Why speakest thou not? Ah, Viṭṭhal, why
Thus silent? Whither shall I fly?

Who else will bear my sore distress?
Smite me not in my helplessness.

As to the child is wholly sweet
His mother,—so to me thy feet.

Thou gracious Lord of Rakhumāī,[1]
Friend of the poor, hear Nāma's cry.

XVII. SEEKING

(*Āvaṭe, 391. Tatva pusāvayā gelo vedajñāsī*)

From Vedic students first the truth I sought,
And found them full of "Thou shalt," "Thou shalt not."
Never shall they possess tranquillity,
For mighty in them is the power of "me."[2]

From Scripture scholars sought I once again
The form divine, but found them rent in twain.
Not one agrees with what the others say,
But pride and error lead them all astray.

Next in Purāns[3] I sought that form so fair,
But still, alas, no place of rest was there.
The preachers preach of Brahm but set their mind
On lust, and so true peace they never find.

Ask of the Haridās[4] the way devout;
You'll find in him no faith at all but doubt.
He tells in words the Name's high excellence,
While all the time engrossed with things of sense.

[1] *Rakhumāī*, Rukmiṇī, the wife of Kriṣṇa.

[2] *The power of "me,"* of egoism, which holds one in bondage by preventing identification with the Supreme Spirit. How far here and elsewhere the idea has an ethical implication and approximates to 'selfishness' it is not easy to judge. Cf. pp. 47, 78, 80, etc.

[3] *Purāns*, collections of legendary stories of the gods, which are expounded in the temples by Purāṇiks or preachers.

[4] *Haridās*, a devotee of Kriṣṇa. Praise of the Name of Kriṣṇa is one of the ways of devotion. See Nos. II and V above.

Weary with seeking, here at last am I.
Low at thy feet, O Pāṇḍuraṅg I lie.
My worldly life is full of fears, but thou
('Tis Nāma cries), O save me, save me now.

XVIII. "MY MOTHER THOU"

(*Āvaṭe, 270. Tū mājhī māulī*)

My Mother thou; thy sucking babe am I:
Feed me with love, my Pāṇḍuraṅg,[1] I cry.

I am the calf with thee the mother cow;
Thy milk, my Pāṇḍuraṅg, withold not now.

I am thy fawn, the mother doe thou art;
Rend the world's snare, my Pāṇḍuraṅg, apart.

Thou mother bird and I among thy brood;
O fly, my Pāṇḍuraṅg, and bring me food.

Ah, heart's belovèd, hear thy Nāma say,
On every side thou hedgest up my way.

XIX. THE MEN OF FAITH[2]

(*Āvaṭe, 1449. Ākalpa āyuṣya*)

Long may that happy household live
Who service to my Hari give.

May no temptation bring distress
But all their lives be blessedness;

No wind of self e'er cause them scathe,
My loved ones, Viṣṇu's men of faith.

Blessings be theirs whose lips have sung
The name of Nāma's Pāṇḍuraṅg.

[1] The name of Pāṇḍuraṅg throughout this *abhaṅg* is used in a feminine form. Cf. Nos. XII and XLIII.

[2] This is sung as the closing song in every *bhajan*. See p. 12.

XX. THE REIGN OF PEACE

(*Āvaṭe, 583. Avaghā saṁsāra sukhācā karīna*)

Now all my days with joy I'll fill
  Full to the brim,
With all my heart to Viṭṭhal cling
  And only him.

He will sweep utterly away
  All dole and care ;
And all in sunder shall I rend
  Illusion's snare.

O altogether dear is he
  And he alone,
For all my burden he will take
  To be his own.

Lo, all the sorrow of the world
  Will straightway cease,
And all unending now shall be
  The reign of peace.

For all the bondage he will break
  Of worldly care,
And all in sunder will he rend
  Illusion's snare.

From all my foolish fancies now
  Let me be free.
In Viṭṭhal, Viṭṭhal only is
  Tranquillity.

XXI. "WHO VĀSUDEV IN ALL CAN SEE"

(*Āvaṭe, 1416. Sarvābhūtī pāhe eka Vāsudeva*)

Who Vāsudev[1] in all can see,
  Cleansed from the thought of "I,"
Know that a saint indeed is he ;
  The rest in bondage lie.

[1] *Vāsudev*, Viṣṇu-Kriṣṇa. For the next line see Note on p. 45, and cf. Nos. XVII, LXXVIII, LXXXII.

Wealth to his eyes is only dust:
  Jewels as stones he sees;
Gone from his heart is rage and lust;
  Pardon dwells there, and peace.

He will not for an instant rest
  (Hear what I, Nāma, say),
But Govind's[1] name—of all the best—
  He utters night and day.

XXII. ILLUMINATION

(Āvaṭe, 586. Nidristāce seje sarpa)

One fast asleep can never know
  That to his chamber crawling in
There comes the snake,—and heedless so
  Am I to lure of sense or sin,
Since inward vision to bestow,
  My Keśav has so gracious been.

Alike are gold and dross to me;
  Jewel and common stone, the same.
Now ne'er my soul can harmèd be,
  Walk I in heaven or in the flame.
Since one with final bliss are we,
  Then what is either praise or blame?

[1] *Govind*, Kṛiṣṇa.

JANĀBĀĪ[1]

(14th Century)

XXIII. PUṆḌLIK

(*Āvaṭe, 172. Bhaktā māji agragaṇī*)

To holy Puṇḍlik[2] give
The highest place.
Sages and saints he saved,—
Saved by his grace.

Thou, standing on the brick,[3]
That grace give me,
Who, Puṇḍlik, clasp thy feet,
So lowlily.

XXIV. GRINDING

(*Āvaṭe, 188. Vairāgya abhimāne*)

Dispassion's mill, with earnest mind,
Lo, here grind I,—
While for a handle faith I find
To turn it by.

A handful of past deeds I deem
Grist for the mill,
And grind in the one Soul supreme
My good or ill.

[1] On Janābāī, see p. 16f.

[2] *Puṇḍlik* is a saint who is specially associated with the origin of the worship of Viṭhobā at Paṇḍharpūr.

[3] He who stands on the brick is Viṭhobā, who, according to the legend, stood patiently waiting while Puṇḍlik attended to his parents needs.

All outward form to dust is ground,
All eyes can see,
For 'tis the Lord himself, I've found,
Who grinds for me.

Strange that this god should come and sit.
His servant nigh;
For I've had nought to do with it,
Says Janābāī.

XXV. THE BESETTING GOD

(Āvaṭe, 198. Deva khāte deva pīte)

Of God my meat and drink I make,
God is the bed on which I lie.
God is whate'er I give or take;
God's constant fellowship have I
For God is here and God is there,—
No place that empty is of him.
Yea, lady Viṭhā,[1] I declare,
I fill the world up to the brim.[2]

[1] *Lady Viṭhā*, Viṭhobā in a feminine form. Compare Pāṇḍuraṅg in Nos. XII and XVIII.

[2] For the last line see p. 17.

EKANĀTH

(1548-99)

XXVI. GOD THE KNOWN AND GOD THE UNKNOWN[1]

(*Bhāgavat. XI, 1458ff*)

How sweet the melted ghee when it congeals.
So, when the Hidden One his form reveals,
How glad the seeker feels.

Dark, dark the far Unknown and closed the way
To thought and speech; silent the scriptures; yea,
No word the Vedas say.

Not thus the Manifest. How fair! How near!
Gone is our thirst if only he appear,—
He, to the heart so dear.

The ever perfect, Bliss eternally,
Being and thought,—lo, Govind now is he,
Spring of all sport and glee.

Strength, courage, fame, the lofty spirit,—lo,
All these we see my lower God bestow,
This, Uddhav,[2] thou must know.

My eyes, if but a glimpse of God I get,
Are healed; escaped am I from out life's net;
Cancelled my sensual debt.

In the lamp's light all hidden things appear;
So when I think upon my God so dear
The far-off God is here.

[1] This selection is taken from Ekanāth's commentary on the 11th chapter of the *Bhāgavata Purāṇa*. For this poet see Introduction, p. 23.

[2] *Uddhav*, the friend of Kṛiṣṇa to whom the 11th chapter of the *Bhāgavata Purāṇa* is addressed by Kṛiṣṇa.

XXVII. THE NINEFOLD PATH OF BHAKTI

(*Navavidhā bhakti nava ācarati*)

Now hearken while we sing their praise
Who follow *bhakti's* ninefold ways.
But name them with the rising sun,—
Thy sins are burned up everyone.

The hearing ear saved Bhūpatī;
In seven days was he set free.
The mighty Bhāgavat to hear
He made himself one listening ear.

Śrī Śuka tried the *kīrtan*,—so
He, too, was saved, as all men know.

The name was chanted by Pralhād
Till truth shone forth and made him glad.
Hari himself came down to men
And slew the demon, Daitya, then.

Ramā was dear unto the Lord,
For she the feet divine adored.
Her soft hands tend with ceaseless care
Those lotus feet, so fine, so fair.

When he the Cowherd's footprints sees
Akrūra falls upon his knees,
And prostrate thus he sings his praise,
Lost in a rapture of amaze.

Sītā exalted Mārutī,
Serving his master lowlily.
The humble service of a slave
To Sītā's lord he gladly gave.

Next Arjun, of the Lord's own kin,
Whom to his heart he gathered in
And taught the Gītā's way of peace,
To find from birth and death release.

Kṛiṣṇa,—himself when Balī gave,—
Before his door served as a slave;
Three paces all the land he sought,
Contented with a beggar's lot.

Now *Bhakti's* ninefold[1] path behold,
By which nine saints attained of old.
Say I,—to render up the soul,
Yea that is *bhakti's* highest goal.

XXVIII. THE SCORNER[2]

(*Bhāvārtha Rāmāyaṇa, Chap. I*)

Who praises and who scorns me too,
Both are my mother. Ay, I view
My scorners as my mother true.

For such are kind to me. They say
Hard words that wash my soil away,
As does a mother's bathing. They

Are friends indeed and strength supply
To me. Were I to blame them, why,
The guilty one would then be I.

O sweet is scorning, setting free
From bondage of duality.
A gracious benefactor he.

Before the scorner bow we low.
Blest be his mother; for I know
Who suffer scorn to Freedom go.

[1] The nine ways of *bhakti*, enumerated (with one omission) above, are as follows:

(1) *Śravaṇa*, or hearing, illustrated by Bhūpatī.
(2) The *Kīrtan*, or singing of sacred songs, illustrated by Śrī Śuka.
(3) *Nāma Smaraṇa*, repetition of the divine name, illustrated by Pralhād.
(4) *Padasevana*, worshipping the feet, illustrated by Ramā.
(5) *Arcana*, worship of an image, is omitted from Ekanāth's enumeration.
(6) *Vandana*, reverential adoration, illustrated by Akrūra.
(7) *Dāsya*, the service of a slave, illustrated by Mārutī.
(8) *Sakhya*, friendship, illustrated by Arjuṇa.
(9) *Ātmanivedana*, self surrender, illustrated by Baḷī.

[2] This is from another work of Ekanāth, his *Bhāvārtha Rāmāyaṇa*.

XXIX. MEN'S REVILING

(*Nindaka kāmācā kāmācā*)

Vile, vile of conduct me they call,
Me, servant of the soul of all.

Vile is my Gaṅga[1] next they say,
Which sweeps my sins all, all away.

Vile is my friend who all for nought
Cleanses my robe of every spot.

Yea, vile my *guru*,[2] he who hath
Made great Janārdan's Ekanāth.

XXX. "GOD DWELLS IN ALL"

(*Deva sarvāṭhāyī vase*)

God dwells in all, and yet we find,
To him the faithless man is blind.

Water or stones or what you will,—
What is it that he does not fill?

Lo, God is present everywhere,
Yet faithless eyes see nothing there.

If Ekanāth unfaithful be,
Then God he also shall not see.

XXXI. THE SPIRITUAL PAṆḌHARĪ.

The body's Paṇḍharī and, dwelling there,
Viṭṭhal, the soul, that being past compare;
  While Bhimā's[3] waters flow with faith and love,
And over all shines Pāṇḍuraṅg[4] the fair.

[1] *Gaṅga*, the sacred river Ganges.
[2] *Guru*, spiritual preceptor, who in Ekanāth's case was Janārdan
[3] *Bhimā*, the river upon which Paṇḍharī or Paṇḍharpūr stands.
[4] *Paṇḍuraṅg*, see Note on p. 43 above.

And mercy, patience, peace are Bhīmā's sand,
Where, rank on rank, the Vaiṣṇav pilgrims stand.
Ah, listen how the music sweetly sounds,—
Joy, worship, truth, and hearts that understand.

My senses form a single company
Of festal worshippers; and lo, I see,—
I, Ekanāth, the pilgrim,—everywhere,
In crowds, in solitude, my Paṇḍharī.

XXXII. "SAINTS GREAT OF HEART"

(*Udār tuhmī santa*)

Saints great of heart and kind are ye,
Fathers and mothers unto me.

So great the blessings you bestow,
How can I praise you, I so low?

For you have saved us, you have showed
To us, dull men, the proper road.

My debt, I, Senā barber,[1] say,
Ah, never, never can I pay.

[1] *Senā*, a barber by caste, was one of Rāmānanda's disciples. Some Marāthī *abhangs* are attributed to him.

TUKĀRĀM[1]

(1608-49)

XXXIII. THE MOTHER'S HOUSE[2]

(*I.P. 266. Kanyā sāsuryāsi jaye*)

As the bride looks back to her mother's house,
And goes, but with dragging feet;
So my soul looks up unto thee and longs,
That thou and I may meet.

As a child cries out and is sore distressed,
When its mother it cannot see,
As a fish that is taken from out the wave,
So 'tis, says Tukā, with me.

XXXIV. THE SUPPLIANT

(*I.P. 530. Ucita te kāya*)

How can I know the right,—
So helpless I—
Since thou thy face hast hid from me,
O thou most high![3]

I call and call again
At thy high gate.
None hears me; empty is the house
And desolate.

[1] For some account of Tukārām see pp. 18ff.

[2] Here Tukārām compares himself in this *saṁsāra*, this condition of "wandering" and exile, which is life in its repeated forms, to the child-bride going to live with her husband and looking back with longing to her mother's house. The mother's house, *māherghar*, round which in India so many happy associations cluster, is for the soul the breast of God. The exiled spirit looks back "to God, who is his home."

[3] Another and perhaps better authenticated interpretation would be:

How can I know the right,—
I, helpless one!
Of pride of knowledge, lo, O God,
I now have none!

If but before thy door
  A guest appear,
Thou'lt speak to him some fitting word,
  Some word of cheer.

Such courtesy, O Lord,
  Becometh thee,
And we,—ah, we're not lost to sense
  So utterly.

XXXV. A BEGGAR FOR LOVE

(*I.P. 1502. Ṭhākalose dvārī*)

A beggar at thy door,
  Pleading I stand;
Give me an alms, O God,
  Love from thy loving hand.

Spare me the barren task,
  To come, and come for nought.
A gift poor Tukā craves,
  Unmerited, unbought.

XXXVI. "GOD WHO IS OUR HOME"

(*I.P. 1820. Mātevinа bāḷā*)

To the child how dull the Fair
If his mother be not there!

So my heart apart from thee,
O thou Lord of Paṇḍharī![1]

Chātak[2] turns from stream and lake,
Only rain his thirst can slake.

How the lotus all the night
Dreameth, dreameth of the light!

[1] *Lord of Paṇḍharī*, that is, Viṭhobā, whose central shrine is a Paṇḍharpūr.

[2] *Chātak*, a species of cuckoo, often called the brain fever bird. It is popularly believed to be able to drink only rain water, and hence its agonised cry for rain.

As the stream to fishes thou,
As is to the calf the cow.

To a faithful wife how dear
Tidings of her Lord to hear!

How a miser's heart is set
On the wealth he hopes to get!

Such, says Tukā, such am I!
But for thee I'd surely die.

XXXVII. THE STRIFE OF SENSE

(*I.P 827. Avaghā veñcalo*)

Wearied by strife of sense,
By call and counter-call,
To thee I hie me thence,
And tell thee all.

Yea, Lord, thou knowest this;
I've brought my life to thee.
Cast down my burden is
And I am free!

Now all my being yearns,
Yearns with a strong desire,
My love within me burns,
A wasting fire.

If thou canst help indeed—
(Hear what I, Tukā, say)—
Nārāyaṇ,[1] help with speed,
Make no delay!

XXXVIII. WAITING

(*I.P. 469. Vāṭa pāhe bāhe*)

With head on hand before my door,
I sit and wait in vain.
Along the road to Paṇḍharī
My heart and eyes I strain.

[1] *Nārāyaṇ*, that is, Viṣṇu. The name probably retains a general suggestion as describing the Supreme Being, though it was appropriated by the Vaiṣṇavas as a name of Viṣṇu.

When shall I look upon my Lord ?
When shall I see him come ?
Of all the passing days and hours
I count the heavy sum.

With watching long my eyelids throb,
My limbs with sore distress,
But my impatient heart forgets
My body's weariness.

Sleep is no longer sweet to me ;
I care not for my bed ;
Forgotten are my house and home,
All thirst and hunger fled.

Says Tukā, Blest shall be the day,—
Ah, soon may it betide !—
When one shall come from Paṇḍharī[1]
To summon back the bride.

XXXIX. DESOLATION

(*I.P. 1836. Ḍoḷiyā pājhar kaṇṭha mājhā dāṭe*)

Sobs choke my throat ; my eyes
Are wet with tears,—
Still waiting for my Pāṇḍuraṅg,
Till he appears.

So long cast off by thee,
My heart despairs.
Ah, whither hast thou gone, absorbed
In other cares ?

So many tasks and cares
Are thine, while I—
I am forgotten thus, alas,
And left to die.

[1] Tukārām lived in the village of Dehū, while Viṭhobā, whom he worshipped, had his temple at Paṇḍharpūr. In this *abhaṅg*, as in No. XXXIII, he is the child-bride, longing to return to his mother's house.

Pilgrims and saints go past
  To Paṇḍharī,
And many messages they bear
  From me to thee.

Who else but thee would run
  To help my need?
O come to me, my Pāṇḍuraṅg,
  O come with speed.

How long still must I wait,
  To see thy face?
Thou hast forgot thy trembling child,
  Thou full of grace.

Once more remember me,
  I, Tukā, pray.
O come to fetch thy darling home,
  Make no delay.

XL. "THEE, LORD OF PITY, I BESEECH"

(*I.P. 2824. Agā karuṇākarā.*)

Thee, Lord of Pity, I beseech,
  Come speedily and set me free.
Yea, when he hears my piteous speech,
  All eager should Nārāyaṇ[1] be.

Lo, in the empty world apart
  I hearken, waiting thy footfall:
Viṭṭhal,[2] thou father, mother art,
  Thou must not loiter at my call.

Thou, thou alone art left to me
All else when weighed is vanity.
Now, Tukā pleads, thy gift of grace complete;
Now let mine eyes behold thy equal feet.

[1] *Nārāyaṇ*, see Note on p. 58 above.

[2] *Viṭṭhal*, one of the names of Viṭhobā or Pāṇḍuraṅg or Kṛiṣṇa.

XLI. FROM THE DEPTHS

(I.P. 3653. Aike Pāṇḍuraṅgā vacana)

O Pāṇḍuraṅg, this once
  Hark to my cry,
For I thy servant am,
  Thine only I.

Save me by whatso means
  Thou best may'st deem ;
No longer now I make
  Or plan or scheme.

How carefully my plans
  And schemes I wrought !
My falsehood and my pride
  Bring all to nought.

One dull of wit am I,
  Of low degree,
By selfishness possessed
  And vanity.

An instant and on me
  Ruin may fall.
Come to my help, O God,
  Come to my call.

XLII. FORSAKE ME NOT !

(I.P. 4381. Kuraṅgī pāḍasa cukalese)

If far from home the poor faun roam,
  With grief its heart will break.
Thus lonely I with thee not nigh
  O do not me forsake !

Thy heart within, all, all my sin
  Ah, hide ; make no delay.
Eternal thou — look on me now
  In love, I, Tukā, pray.

XLIII. MOTHER VIṬHOBĀ

(*I.P. 1540. Tuja mhaṇatila kṛipecā sāgara*)

Ah, Pāṇḍuraṅg, if, as men say,
  A sea of love thou art,
Then wherefore dost thou so delay?
  O take me to thy heart !

I cry for thee as for the hind
  The faun makes sore lament.
Nowhere its mother it can find,
  With thirst and hunger spent.

With milk of love, ah, suckle me
  At thy abounding breast,
O Mother, haste.—In thee, in thee
  My sad heart findeth rest.

XLIV. ME MISERABLE

(*I.P. 806. Alpa mājhī matī*)

Since little wit have I,
O hear my mournful cry.

Grant now, O grant to me
That I thy feet may see.

I have no steadfastness,
Nārāyaṇ,[2] I confess.

Have mercy, Tukā prays,
On my unhappy case.

XLV. WITHIN MY HEART

(*I.P. 868. Na kaḷatā kāya*)

I know no way by which
My faith thy feet can reach
  Nor e'er depart.

[1] In this *abhaṅg* the conception of Viṭhobā or Pāṇḍuraṅg as a mother, which we have already met with (see Note on p. 43 above), is elaborated.

[2] *Nārāyaṇ*, see Note on p. 58 above.

How, how can I attain
That thou, O Lord, shalt reign
Within my heart?

Lord, I beseech thee, hear
And grant to faith sincere,
My heart within,
Thy gracious face to see,
Driving afar from me
Deceit and sin.

O come, I, Tukā, pray,
And ever with me stay,
Mine, mine to be.
Thy mighty hand outstretch
And save a fallen wretch,
Yea, even me.

XLVI. THE RESTLESS HEART

(I.P. 1031. Jivanāvacūni taḷamaḷī māsā)

As on the bank the poor fish lies
And gasps and writhes in pain,
Or as a man with anxious eyes
Seeks hidden gold in vain,—
So is my heart distressed and cries
To come to thee again.

Thou knowest, Lord, the agony
Of the lost infant's wail,
Yearning his mother's face to see.
(How oft I tell this tale!)
O at thy feet the mystery
Of the dark world unveil!

The fire of this harassing thought
Upon my bosom preys.
Why is it I am thus forgot?
(O, who can know thy ways?)
Nay, Lord, thou seest my hapless lot;
Have mercy, Tukā says.

XLVII. "I LONG TO SEE THY FACE"

(*I.P. 2672. Tuja pāhāve he dharito vāsanā*)

I long to see thy face,
But ah, in me hath holiness no place.
By thy strength succour me,
So only, only I thy feet may see!
Though Sādhu's[1] robes I've worn,
Within I'm all unshaven and unshorn.
Lost, lost, O God, am I,
Unless thou help me, Tukā,—me who cry!

XLVIII. "KEEP ME FROM VANITY"

(*I.P. 3443. Nako maja tāṭhā, nako abhimāna*)

Keep me from vanity
  Keep me from pride,
For sure I perish if
  I quit thy side.
From this deceiving world
  How hard to flee!
Ah, thou, Vaikuṇṭha's[2] Lord,
  Deliver me!
If once thy gracious face
  I look upon,
The world's enticement then
  Is past and gone.

XLIX. ASPIRATION

(*I.P. 1996. Devā ātā aisā kari upakāra*)

One favour grant, O God,—that now by me
  My flesh may be forgot;
So shall I have (for I at last have learned)
  Bliss for my lot.

[1] *Sādhu*, an ascetic who, as such, wears a yellow robe and shaves his head.

[2] *Vaikuṇṭha*, the heaven of Viṣṇu, or Kṛiṣṇa or Viṭhobā.

Give to my heart and all its moods a place
Close by thy side ;
Break, break the bond that binds me to desire,
To passion, shame and pride.

Thy name to utter and the saints to know,—
I beg but this of thee.
Here is no feigning, Lord ; my service take
Of faith and purity !

L. THE ONLY REFUGE

(*I.P. 4004. Avaghyā pātakāñcī mī eka rāśī*)

I am a mass of sin ;
Thou art all purity ;
Yet thou must take me as I am
And bear my load for me.
Me Death has all consumed ;
In thee all power abides.
All else forsaking, at thy feet
Thy servant Tukā hides.

LI. DESOLATE

(*I.P. 3695. Koṇāçecintana karā aiśā kāḷe*)

When thought of all but thee
Has from me gone,
Still by thy strength upheld
I struggle on.

Come to me, Viṭṭhal,[1] come !
For thee I wait.
O, wherefore hast thou me
Left desolate.

Many oppress me sore
With cruel might ;
My very enemies
Are day and night.

[1] *Viṭṭhal*, see Note on p. 40 above.

Ah come and take thy place
At my heart's core ;
Then shall the net of ill
Snare me no more.

LII. "O SAVE ME, SAVE ME!"

(*I.P.* 3837. *Trāhe, trāhe, trāhe, soḍavī anantā*)

O save me, save me, Mightiest,
Save me and set me free.
O let the love that fills my breast
Cling to thee lovingly.

Grant me to taste how sweet thou art ;
Grant me but this, I pray,
And never shall my love depart
Or turn from thee away.

Then I thy name shall magnify
And tell thy praise abroad,
For very love and gladness I
Shall dance before my God.

Grant to me, Viṭṭhal,[1] that I rest
Thy blessed feet beside ;
Ah, give me this, the dearest, best,
And I am satisfied.

LIII. NEAR YET FAR

(*I.P.* 4419. *Tujaviṇa tiḷabharī*)

There is no place, small as a sesamum,
But thou, they say, art there.
That deep in all this universe thou dwell'st
Sages and saints declare.

So, I, of old thy child, in faith of this
Come seeking help from thee.
Thou overflow'st the world, and yet, and yet,
Thy face I cannot see.

[1] *Viṭṭhal*, see Note on p. 40 above.

"Why should I meet this abject—I to whom
There is nor bound nor end?"
Is it with such a thought thou comest not,
My father and my friend?
Ah, what shall Tuka do that he thy feet
May touch and tend?

LIV. BEYOND THE MOUNTAINS, GOD

(*I.P. 4420. Kāma krodha āḍa*)

Here tower the hills of passion and of lust,—
Far off the Infinite!
No path I find and all impassable
Fronts me the hostile height.

Ah, God is lost, my friend. Nārāyaṇ[1] now
How can I e'er attain?
Thus it appears that all my life, so dear,
I've spent, alas, in vain.

LV. "I CANNOT UNDERSTAND: I LOVE"

(*I.P. 4361. Na kaḷe mahimā*)

Thy greatness none can comprehend·
All dumb the Vedas are.
Forspent the powers of mortal mind;
They cannot climb so far.
How can I compass him whose light
Illumes both sun and star?

The serpent of a thousand tongues[2]
Cannot tell all thy praise;
Then how, poor I? Thy children we,
Mother of loving ways!
Within the shadow of thy grace,
Ah, hide me, Tukā says.

[1] *Nārāyaṇ*, see Note on p. 58 above. The name appears to be used here to suggest the Supreme Being, above man's reach.

[2] *The serpent of a thousand tongues*, Śeṣa, the thousand-headed snake which is at once the couch and canopy of Viṣṇu and which upholds the world.

LVI. NOT ONE BUT TWO

(I.P. 3753. Advaitī to mājhe nāhī samādhāna)

Advait[1] contents me not, but dear to me
  The service of thy feet.
O grant me this reward! To sing of thee
  To me how sweet!

Setting us twain, lover and Lord, apart,
  This joy to me display.
Grant it to Tukā—Lord of all thou art—
  Some day, some day.

LVII. MAN'S EXTREMITY[2]

(I.P. 648. Mājhā tava khuṇṭalā upāva)

Ah, then, O God, the efforts all are vain
By which I've sought thy blessed feet to gain.
  First there was loving faith, but faith I've none;
Nowise my restless soul can I restrain.

Then pious deeds, but no good will have I
For these; nor wealth to help the poor thereby;
  I know not how to honour Brāhman guests;
Alas! the springs of love in me are dry.

I cannot serve the *guru* or the saint;
Not mine to chant the name, with toil to faint,
  Perform the sacred rites, renounce the world.
I cannot hold my senses in restraint.

[1] *Advait*, the philosophical doctrine of non-duality, that is, of the ultimate identity of the individual soul and the Supreme Soul. Tukārām prefers " the bliss of duality."

[2] The poet here enumerates various means by which the divine favour is sought or by which men endeavour to obtain Release. These vary from the feeding of Brāhmans to attainment of a condition of unity with Brahman beyond all distinctions. He finds himself unequal to any of them and finally casts himself upon God's mercy. For a similar testimony on the part of Nāmdev see No. XVII above.

My heart has never trod the pilgrim's way;
The vows I make I know not how to pay.
"Ah, God is here," I cry. Not so, not so.[1]
For me distinctions have not passed away.

Therefore, I come, O God, to plead for grace,
I, worthy only of a servant's place.
No store of merit such an one requires.
My firm resolve is taken, Tukā says.

LVIII. THOUGH HE SLAY ME

(I.P. 626. Ātā tuja kaḷela te karī)

Now I submit me to thy will,
Whether thou save or whether kill;
Keep thou me near or send me hence,
Or plunge me in the war of sense.[2]

Thee in my ignorance I sought,
Of true devotion knowing nought.
Little could I, a dullard, know,
Myself the lowest of the low.

My mind I cannot steadfast hold;
My senses wander uncontrolled.
Ah, I have sought and sought for peace.
In vain; for me there's no release.

Now bring I thee a faith complete
And lay my life before thy feet.
Do thou, O God, what seemeth best;
In thee, in thee alone is rest.

In thee I trust, and, hapless wight,
Cling to thy skirts with all my might.
My strength is spent, I, Tukā say;
Now upon thee this task I lay.

[1] "*Ah God is here.*" He has not attained to a realisation of his identity with the Supreme Spirit, or, perhaps, he has not realised God's presence.

[2] *War of sense, saṁsāra,* "wandering," rebirth again and again in the body.

LIX. PĀṆḌURAṄG

(*I.P. 1033. Koṇa āhmā puse*)

Who asks if spent and weary we?
Who else, O Pāṇḍuraṅg, but thee?

Whom shall we tell our joy or grief?
Who to our thirst will bring relief?

Who else this fever will assuage?
Who bear us o'er the ocean's rage?

Who will our heart's desire impart
And clasp us to his loving heart?

What other master shall we own?
What helper else but thee alone?

Ah, Tukā says, thou knowest all,
Prostrate before thy feet I fall.

LX. COMPLETE SURRENDER

(*I.P. 702. Āṇika dusare maja nāhī*)

Now Pāṇḍuraṅg I've chosen for my part,
None, none but his to be.
In all my thoughts he dwells, dwells in my heart,
Sleeping and waking he.

Yea, all my being's powers before him bow;
None other faith is aught.
See, Tukā says, mine eyes behold him now,
Standing all wrapt in thought.[1]

LXI. TO THY DEAR FEET!

(*I.P. 4161. Prema jaḍale*)

To thy dear feet my love I bind:
No other longing stirs my mind.

[1] *Standing all wrapt in thought.* Compare the description on p. 49 above, of this god as "standing on the brick."

I think of thee through days and nights,
And so discharge my holy rites.

Nought know I but thy name alone :—
Thus to myself myself am known.

When comes at last the hour of death
O save me, save me, Tukā saith.

LXII. HE LEADETH ME

(*I.P. 2000. Jethe jāto tethe tū*)

Holding my hand thou leadest me,
  My comrade everywhere.
As I go on and lean on thee,
  My burden thou dost bear.

If, as I go, in my distress
  I frantic words should say,
Thou settest right my foolishness
  And tak'st my shame away.

Thus thou to me new hope dost send,
  A new world bringest in ;
Now know I every man a friend
  And all I meet my kin.

So like a happy child I play
  In thy dear world, O God,
And everywhere—I, Tukā, say—
  Thy bliss is spread abroad.

LXIII. THE JOY OF THE NAME

(*I.P. 818. Nāmā āṭhavitā*)

Lord, let it be that when thy name
  Into my thoughts shall come,
My love to thee shall mount like flame,
  My lips with joy be dumb.

Filled are my eyes with happy tears,
  With rapture every limb ;
Yea, with thy love my frame appears
  Filled to the very brim.

Thus all my body's strength I'll spend
In hymns of joyful praise;
Thy name I'll sing nor ever end
Through all the nights and days.

Yea, Tukā says, for ever so
I'll do, for this is best,
Since at the feet of saints, I know,
Is found eternal rest.

LXIV. LOVE'S CAPTIVE

(*I.P. 783. Premasūtra dorī*)

Bound with cords of love I go,
By Hari[1] captive led,
Mind and speech and body, lo,
To him surrenderèd.

He shall rule my life for he
Is all compassionate.
His is sole authority,
And we his will await.

LXV. THE BHAKTA'S DUTY

(*I.P. 1437. Niṣṭhāvantā bhāva*)

The duty of the man of faith
Is trust and loyalty,
A purpose hid within his heart
That cannot movèd be.

A steadfast faith and passionless
In Viṭṭhal that abides,
A faith that not an instant strays
To any god besides.

Who that is such a one as that
Was ever cast away?
Never has such a tale been told,
Never, I, Tukā, say.

[1] *Harī*, that is, Kṛiṣṇa.

LXVI. LOVE FINDS OUT GOD

(*I.P. 810. Manavācātīta tujhe he svarūpa*)

Thy nature is beyond the grasp
  Of human speech or thought.
So love[1] I've made the measure-rod,
  By which I can be taught.

Thus with the measure-rod of love
  I mete the Infinite.
In sooth, to measure him there is
  None other means so fit.

Not *Yoga's*[2] power, nor sacrifice,
  Nor fierce austerity,
Nor yet the strength of thought profound
  Hath ever found out thee.

And so, says Tukā, graciously,
  Oh Keśav,[3] take, we pray
Love's service that with simple hearts
  Before thy feet we lay.

LXVII. "GOD IS OURS"

(*I.P. 1870. Deva āmacā āmacā*)

God is ours, yea, ours is he,
Soul of all the souls that be.

God is nigh without a doubt,
Nigh to all, within, without.

God is gracious, gracious still;
Every longing he'll fulfil.

God protects, protects his own;
Strife and death he casteth down.

Kind is God, ah, kind indeed;
Tukā he will guard and lead.

[1] *Love*, *bhakti* or loving devotion. See Introduction, p. 11.
[2] *Yoga*, see note on p. 36 above. [3] *Keśav*, Kriṣṇa.

LXVIII. "ONE THING I DO"

(*I.P. 2638. Laukikā puratī nahve mājhī sevā*)

I serve thee, not because
  Honour I crave;
Nay, Keśav,[1] for I am
  Thy slave.

Therefore to serve thy feet,—
  For this I cry;
For naught, for naught but this
  Crave I.

To my Lord's service, see,
  One heart I've brought,
Ever,—without, within,—
  One thought.

Thus mine appointed task
  Do I somehow;
Whether 'tis wrong or right
  Judge thou.

LXIX. HE KNOWS OUR NEEDS

(*I.P. 602. Trailokya pāḷitā*)

Unwearied he bears up the universe;
  How light a burden I!
Does not his care the frog within the stone
  With food supply?

The bird, the creeping thing, lays up no store;
  This great One knows their need.
And if I, Tukā, cast on him my load,
  Will not his mercy heed?

[1] *Keśav*, one of the names of Kṛiṣṇa.

LXX. "IN HIM ABIDE"

(*I.P. 819. Jananī he jaṇe bāḷakāce varma*)

The mother knows her child,—his secret heart,
His joy or woe.
Who holds the blind man's hand alone can tell
Where he desires to go.
The timid suppliant at his champion's back
Can safely hide.
Who only clings, see, the strong swimmer bears
To the stream's further side.
Viṭṭhal, says Tukā, knows our every need;
Only in him abide.

LXXI. THE BOLDNESS OF FAITH

(*I.P. 716. Bhavasindhūce kāya kode*)

Launch upon the sea of life;
Fear not aught that thou mayst meet.
Stout the ship of Pāṇḍuraṅg;
Not a wave shall wet thy feet.
Many saints await thee there,
Standing on the further shore:
Haste, says Tukā, haste away,
Follow those who've gone before.

LXXII. BEATA CULPA

(*I.P. 758. Jari mī nahvto patita*)

How couldst thou e'er have cleansèd me,
But for my sinful plight?
So first come I, and then thy grace,
O mercy infinite.
The magic stone[1] was nothing worth,
Till iron brought it fame.
Did no one by the Wish Tree[2] wish,
Whence would it get its name?

[1] *The magic stone*, *parisa*, which turns iron into gold.
[2] *The Wish Tree*, *kalpataru*, a tree in Indra's heaven, supposed to grant every desire. Compare the *kāmadhenu*, the cow of plenty, which has a similar property.

LXXIII. THE SNARE OF PRIDE

(*I.P. 1779 Vacecyā cāpalye*)

None skilled as I in craft of subtle speech ;
But, ah, the root of things I cannot reach.

Therefore, O Lord of Paṇḍharī, my heart
Is sore distressed. Who knows my inward part ?

I proud became from honour that men paid
To me,—and thus my upward growth was stayed.

Alas ! The way of truth I cannot see,
Held fast by Self in dark captivity.

LXXIV. I AM POOR AND NEEDY

(*I.P. 764. Kriyāmatihīna*)

No deeds I've done nor thoughts I've thought ;
Save as thy servant, I am nought.

Guard me, O God, and O, control
The tumult of my restless soul.

Ah, do not, do not cast on me
The guilt of mine iniquity.

My countless sins, I, Tukā, say,
Upon thy loving heart I lay.

LXXV. A BLIND LEADER OF THE BLIND

(*I.P. 1001. Catura mī jālo*)

I have grown very wise
In mine own foolish eyes,
  But faith has fled.
My life is vain indeed ;
But worse that rage and greed
  Dwell in faith's stead.

The world's possessed by sin
And envy reigns within
  The human breast ;
And I shall teach mankind,
Though I'm myself as blind
  As all the rest.

LXXVI. THE PRIDE OF KNOWLEDGE

(*I.P. 2849. Hīṇa mājhī yātī*)

Though I'm a man of lowly birth
The saints have magnified my worth.

And so within my heart to hide
Has come the great destroyer, pride.

In my fond heart the fancy dwells
That I am wise and no one else.

O, save me, save me, Tukā prays ;
Spent like the wind are all my days.

LXXVII. THE UNVEILING OF LOVE

(*I.P. 2966. Jāṇoni neṇate karī mājhe mana*)

Enlighten thou mine eyes
Making me lowly wise ;
    Thy love to me unveil.
Then in the world I'll be
As, from all soilure free,
    The lotus pure and pale.

Whether men praise or jeer,
Hearing I shall not hear ;
    Like the rapt *yogī*[1] I.
To me the world shall seem
Like visions of a dream
    That, with our waking, fly.

Till we that state attain
All, all our toil is vain,
    I, Tukā, testify.

[1] *Yogī*, see Note on p. 36 above.

LXXVIII. THE HAVEN

(*I.P. 3696. Kāji tuhmī aise nahva kṛipāvanta*)

Ah, wherefore so unkind ?
  Let my sad breast
At the hid centre find
  It's place of rest.

No wind of good or ill
  Shall enter there,
But peace, supremely still,
  Supremely fair.

To me the flux of things
  Brings sore distress ;
The world's mutation brings
  But heaviness.

Therefore I, Tukā, cry,
  Clinging thy feet,
"Break, break my 'me' and 'my,'[1]
  My vain conceit."

LXXIX. WEARINESS

(*I.P. 977. Kāya ātā āhmī poṭa ci bharāve*)

Shall we, sham saints, the world beguile
Glutting our belly's greed the while ?

O tell thy thought, if this it be,
For I am weary utterly.

Shall we the poet's mood rehearse
And string together endless verse ?

Shall Tukā ope his shop[2] again
And, O Nārāyaṇ, ruin men ?

[1] *My "me" and "my,"* see Note on p. 45 above.
[2] *His shop.* Tukārām was a seller of grain.

LXXX. GOD'S COUNTERFEIT

(*I.P. 347. Je kā rañjale gāñjale*)

Is there a man who says of all,
Whether upon them sorrow fall,
Or whether joy—"These, these are mine"?
That is the saint: mark well the sign.
God dwells in him. The good man's breast
Is of all men's the tenderest.
Is any helpless or undone?
Be he a slave, be he a son:—
On all alike he mercy shows,
On all an equal love bestows.

How oft must I this tale repeat!
That man is God's own counterfeit.

LXXXI. SELF-SURRENDER

(*I.P. 3474. Dilā jīvabhāva*)

My self I've rendered up to thee;
I've cast it from me utterly.

Now here before thee, Lord, I stand,
Attentive to thy least command.

The self within me now is dead,
And thou enthronèd in its stead.

Yea, this I, Tukā, testify,
No longer now is "me" or "my."

LXXXII. DYING TO LIVE[1]

(*I.P. 2668. Āpule maraṇa pāhile myā doḷā*)

Before my eyes my dead self lies;
  O, bliss beyond compare!
Joy fills the worlds, and I rejoice,
  The soul of all things there.

[1] This is one of Tukārām's *abhangs* which is interpreted differently by those who claim him as a theist and those who claim him as a

My selfish bonds are loosed, and now
I reach forth far and free.
Gone is the soil of birth and death,
The petty sense of "me."

Nārāyaṇ's grace gave me this place,
Where I in faith abide.
Now, Tukā says, my task I've done
And spread the message wide.

LXXXIII. THE ROOT OF LONGING

(*I.P. 1436. Āśā he samūla khaṇoni kāḍhāvī*)

Who is he would act the true *gosavī's*[1] part?
Let him dig the root of longing from his heart.
If he dare not, in his pleasures let him stay—
Folly were it should he choose another way.
For when longing he hath slain victoriously,
Only then shall he from all come forth set free.
Yea, says Tukā, does thy heart for union thirst?
Crush—be sure!—the seed of longing in thee first.

LXXXIV. THE SECRET OF PEACE

(*I.P. 580. Śāntīparate nāhī sukha*)

Calm[2] is life's crown; all other joy beside
Is only pain.
Hold thou it fast, thou shalt, whate'er betide,
The further shore attain.

When passions rage and we are wrung with woe
And sore distress,
Comes calm, and then—yea, Tukā knows it—lo!
The fever vanishes.

follower of *advaita* pantheism. To the former it seems that the bliss he describes is that which comes from the death of the lower self and the presence of God in his heart. To the latter the bliss is that which is produced by the realisation of his identity with the Supreme Spirit, and the "self-naughting" is the disappearance of personality itself.

[1] *Gosavī*, a holy man, usually of the *Śūdra* class, who has renounced the world.

[2] *Calm*, śānti.

LXXXV. THE FELLOWSHIP OF SAINTS

(*I.P. 2051. Agnimājī gele*)

What enters fire, its former nature lost,
Fire to itself transforms.
Touched by the magic stone, lo, iron now
Gold that the world adorns.
Into the Gaṅgā[1] flow the little streams,
With the great Gaṅgā blent.
Nay, e'en its neighbour trees the sandal tree
Infects with its sweet scent.
So to the feet of saints is Tukā bound,
Linked in a blest content.

LXXXVI. THE SIMPLE PATH

(*I.P. 2341. Bahutā chandāce bahu vase jana*)

Diverse men's thoughts as are their vanities,
Distract not thou thy mind to follow these.
Cling to the faith that thou hast learned, the love
That, coming, filled thee with its fragrances.

For Harī's worship is a mother,—rest
It is and peace, shade for the weariest.
Why, then, who ties a stone about his neck
And drowns himself, is but a fool confessed.

LXXXVII. THE WAY OF LOVE

(*I.P. 1589. Ghotavīna lāḷa*)

The learned in Brahma I shall make to long
With new desire; those once so safe and strong,
Set free, I bring back glad to bondage. So,
They are made one with Brahma by a song.[2]

[1] *Gaṅgā*, the river Ganges.

[2] *By a song*, that is, by the *kīrtan*, the method of celebrating the praise of the god by music and singing. This is one of the chief methods of *bhakti*, as followed by Tukārām, and he praises it as more effective than the way of knowledge followed by the philosopher or than any other way. See Introduction, p. 24.

God is their debtor[1] now, O glad release.
I'll bid the weary pilgrim take his ease.
The proud ascetic may forsake his pride.
Away with offerings and charities!

By love and true devotion life's high goal
I'll help men to attain—yea, Brahma's soul.[2]
"O, happy we, who Tukā's face have seen"—
So men will say and Tukā they'll extol.

LXXXVIII. THE THIEF

(*I.P. 4265. Jālo balivanta hōūniyā Śaraṇāgata*)

I came to him in woful plight;
He, gracious, girded me with might.

His house I entered unaware
And stole the treasure hidden there.

So I have wrought a deep design
That all his riches shall be mine.

I kissed his feet and then by stealth
I, Tukā, robbed him of his wealth.

LXXXIX. THE TRAVELLER

(*I.P. 3189. Kṣaṇakṣaṇā hācī karāvā vicāra*)

Let thy thought at all times be,—
Over life's tempestuous sea
  We must fare.
Soon the body perisheth;
Life is swallowed up of Death.
  O beware!

Seek the fellowship of saints;
Seek, until thy spirit faints,
  Heaven's ways!
Let not dust make blind thine eyes,
Dust of worldly enterprise,
  Tukā says.

[1] *God is their debtor*, because he desires, and gets from them, love.
[2] *Brahma's soul*, the real essence of Brahma, which is the goal of all Hindu religious effort.

XC. BY FAITH ALONE

(*I.P. 949 Āṭhave deva*)

In God, in God—forget him not!—
Do thou thy refuge find.
Let every other plan or plot
Go with the wind!

Why toil for nought? Wake, wake from sleep!
By learning's load weighed down,
Thou in the world's abysses deep
Art like to drown.

O, flee from thence. Only by faith
Canst thou to God attain.
And all thy knowledge, Tukā saith,
Will prove in vain.

XCI. A STEADFAST MIND

(*I.P. 109. Māna apamāna gove*)

Honour, dishonour that men may pay,
Bundle them up and throw them away.

Where there is ever a steadfast mind,
There thou the vision of God shalt find.

Whereso the fountains of peace abide,
Stayed is the passage of time and tide.

Calm thou the impulse that stirs thy breast;
Surely, says Tukā, a small request.

XCII. THE NAME OF THE LIVING ONE

(*I.P. 1462. Devā aike he vinantī*)

Hear, O God, my supplication,—
Do not grant me Liberation.[1]

[1] *Liberation*, *moksa*, *mukti*, absorption in the Supreme Spirit with its consequence that he will not be reborn. He does not wish this gift, but desires to live in the world, experiencing the love of devotion as a Vaiṣṇavite, a follower of *bhakti*. Cf. Note on p. 35 above.

'Tis what men so much desire ;
Yet how much this joy is higher !

Home of every Vaiṣṇavite,
See, with glow of love alight !

By their door with folded hands
Full Attainment waiting stands.

Heavenly joy is not for me,
For it passeth speedily ;

But that name how strangely dear
That in songs of praise we hear !

Yea, thou, dark as clouds[1] that lower,
Knowest not thine own name's power.

Ah, says Tukā, it is this
Makes our lives so full of bliss.

XCIII. THE DEDICATED LIFE

(*I.P. 1368. Nako sodū anna*)

Ah, wherefore fast or wherefore go
To solitude apart?
Whether thou joy or sorrow know
Have God within thy heart.

If in his mother's arms he be
The child knows nought amiss.
Cast out, yea, cast out utterly
All other thought than this.

Love not the world nor yet forsake
Its gifts in fear and hate.
Thy life to God an offering make
And to him dedicate.

Nay, Tukā says, ask not again,
Waking old doubts anew.
Whatever else is taught by men,
None other word is true.

[1] *Dark as clouds*, that is, Kṛiṣṇa, called here Meghaśyāma.

XCIV. THE INWARD PURPOSE

(*I.P. 260. Dharma rakṣāvayāsāṭhī.*)

To keep the Holy Order[1] pure,—
This ever is my purpose sure.

The Vedic statutes I proclaim;
To imitate the saints my aim.

For, with no firm resolve within,
To quit the world is deadly sin.

Vile he who does so, Tukā says,—
Evil the worship that he pays.

XCV. THE BHAKTA'S TASK

(*I.P. 520. Āhmī Vaikuṇṭhavāsī*)

When from Vaikuṇṭha[2] forth we came
This of our coming was the aim—
That what the sages taught we by our lives proclaim.

Since filled the world with sedge and weed,
To sweep the paths our lowly meed,
Trod by the saints, and on their sacred scraps[3] to feed.

Gone the old wisdom, and instead
Mere words that wide have ruin spread.
Lustful men's minds, the way to God quite vanishèd.

Beat we the drum of Love, whose din
Brings terror to this age of sin.
Hail, Tukā bids, with joy the victory we win.

XCVI. MĀYĀ

(*I.P. 300. Mṛigajalā kāya karāvā utāra*)

If the river be a mirage that I see
Then what need for me
Of a ford?

[1] *The Holy Order*, the *Dharma*, the divine society held together by religious law and by the system of caste. Cf. Note on p. 35 above.
[2] *Vaikuṇṭha*, the heaven of Viṣṇu.
[3] *Sacred scraps*, the remains of the sacrifice, or sacred meal, which are consumed by the worshipper or the ministrant.

If the children buy and sell in make-believe,
Who should joy or grieve,
Gain or lose?

Are not maidens still in kinship just the same,
Though they wedded in a game,
Girl with girl?

Joy or sorrow that we meet with in our dreams
To us waking seems
Nothing real.

So, says Tukā, births and dying,—nought is true.
Bondage, freedom too,
Weary me.

XCVII. "THE WORLD PASSETH AWAY"

(*I.P. 2811. Gele paḷāle divasa roza*)

Who dares call aught his own
  As swiftly speed the days?
Time keeps the fatal score,
  And not a moment strays.

Hair, ears, and eyes grow old,
  As, dullard, grow they must;
The best is nigh thee, yet
  Thou fill'st thy mouth with dust.

Dying and yet thou buildst
  As for eternity!
Nay, haste to Pāṇḍuraṅg!
  'Tis Tukā says it: flee!

XCVIII. THE WAY OF DEATH.

(*I.P. 1562. Eka pāhātasā ekāci dahane*)

Ah, friend, beware; see how they bear
  The dead men to the ghaut.[1]
To God on high with agony
  Call and cease not.

[1] *The ghaut*, the burning ghaut where the bodies of the dead are cremated.

Though 'mong the dead not numberèd,
  Within thy scrip is death.
Fill up, fill up with good thy cup,
  While thou hast breath.

List what I say;—the narrow way
  Is dense with dying men;
'Mong them at last thy lot is cast.
  No succour then.

XCIX. "THE NIGHT COMETH"

(*I.P. 2693. Neṇe japatapa anuṣṭhāna yāga*)

Lo, Death draws nigh; and what know I
  Of rite, or vow, or prayer?
To God alone who guards his own
  I flee and hide me there.

The tally's[1] score grows more and more,—
  Then night and all is done.
Hear Tukā say,—dear every day
  From that grim robber won.

C. 'TIS ALL FOR NAUGHT

(*Cāturyāce yoge kavitva karītī*)

With whatso skill he may his verse refine,
'Tis all for naught without the breath divine.

Let him put on the holy beggar's dress;
'Tis all for naught without unworldliness.

He paints the sun or moon upon a wall;
'Tis all for naught without the light of all.

O, he may play, of course, a soldier's part;
'Tis all for naught without a warrior heart.

So, Tukā says, they've danced and songs they've sung,
'Tis naught without the love of Pāṇḍuraṅg.

[1] *The tally.* In counting it is often the custom in India to put aside a piece of wood or other article for each quantity counted, so as to keep the score.

CI. THE DIVINE INSPIRATION

(*I.P. 2949. Āpuliyā baḷe*)

'Tis not I who speak so featly ;
  All my words my Lover's are.
Hark, Sāḷuṅki[1] singing sweetly,
  Taught, as I, by One afar.

How could I, abject, achieve it ?
  'Tis the all-upholding One.
Deep his skill, who can conceive it ?
  He can make the lame to run.

CII. DROWNING MEN

(*I.P. 948. Upakārāsāṭhī bolo he upāya*)

For men's saving I make known
These devices—this alone
My desire.

Can my heart unmovèd be
When before my eyes I see
Drowning men ?

I shall see them with my eyes
When their plight they realise
At the last.

CIII. WITHOUT AND WITHIN

(*I.P. 2869. Ālī siṁhasthparvaṇī*)

Soon as the season of Siṁhasth[2] comes in,
The barber and the priest—what wealth they win !
Thousands of sins may lurk within his heart,
If only he will shave his head and chin !

What is shaved off is gone, but what else, pray ?
What sign that sin is gone ? His evil way
Is still unchanged. Yea, without faith and love
All is but vanity, I, Tukā, say.

[1] *Sāḷuṅki*, a common Indian bird, *gracula religiosa*.

[2] *The season of Siṁhasth*, the period during which the planet Jupiter is in the constellation Leo. "The period is considered favourable for the washing away of sins, and Hindus go to holy places, such as Nasik, shave their heads and moustaches and bathe in the river."—Bhandarkar's *Vaiṣṇavism*, p. 94, Note.

CIV. "AND HAVE NOT CHARITY"

(*I.P. 90. Tiḷa jāḷile tānduḷa*)

Your heart from rage and lust has nowise turned
For all the rice and sesamum[1] you've burned.
You've toiled for naught with learned words whose fruit
Is vain display—and Pāṇḍuraṅg you've spurned.

By pilgrimage and grim austerity
Only your pride has grown ; your "I" and "me"[2]
Swell with your alms ; the secret, Tukā says,
You've missed : your acts are sinful utterly.

CV. THE MENDICANT

(*I.P. 679. Āśābaddha vaktā*)

Lust binds the preacher, fear
The doubting hearts of those his words who hear.

He knows not what he sings :
His mouth he opes for what each comer brings.

A greedy cat, he steals
From door to door, begging from men his meals.

What Tukā says is true ;
The sack is empty and the measure[3] too.

CVI. THE PROUD ADVAITIST

(*I.P. 1471. Naikāve kāni*)

To such pay thou no heed: the words he saith
Are only chaff, empty of loving faith.
He praises high *Advait*[4] which only brings
To speaker and to hearer pain and scaithe.

[1] *Rice and sesamum*, offerings given to gods.
[2] *Your "I" and "me."* See Note on p. 45 above.
[3] *The measure* is a vessel by means of which grain is measured from the heap into the sack.
[4] *Advait*, the doctrine of the identity of the individual soul and the Supreme Soul, which is expressed in the Sanscrit phrase, "Brahmāsmi," "I am Brahm."

The saints are the adherents of the *bhakti* doctrine, which is not, of course, monistic.

He fills his belly saying, "I am Brahm."
Waste not thy words upon him; shamed and dumb
Is he, blasphemer, when he meets the saints.
Who scorns God's love Tukā calls vilest scum.

CVII. THE HYPOCRITE: I

(*I.P. 603. Bolī meindācī*)

His speech—the hypocrite's—is well and fair,
But all his thought is how he can ensnare.

He outwardly appears a godly man;
In truth he is a very ruffian.

His forehead-mark,[1] his beads, a saint denote,
But in the darkness he would cut your throat.

Ay, Tukā says, a very scoundrel he;
The pains of Yama[2] wait him certainly.

CVIII. THE HYPOCRITE: II

(*I.P. 776. Ḍoī vāḍhavūni keśa*)

Possessed with devils they grow long their hair.
No saints are they, nor trace of God they bear.
They tell of omens to a gaping crowd.
Rogues are they, Tukā says; Govind's[3] not there.

[1] *The forehead-mark* indicates the sect to which he belongs, while a rosary of beads is worn round the neck.

[2] *Yama*, the god of the under-world, who punishes the wi.ked.

[3] *Govind*, Kṛiṣṇa.

BIBLIOGRAPHY

The most recent and most authoritative account in English of the Marāṭhā poets is to be found in the Wilson Philological Lectures (1917) of Professor W. B. Patwardhan, of the Fergusson, College, Poona. These have been printed in the *Fergusson College Magazine*, Vol. VIII, Nos. 3 and 4, and Vol. IX, Nos. 1-4. An earlier lecture by Professor Patwardhan, on "Some *Abhaṅgs* of Nāmdev," appeared in the same Magazine, Vol. III, No. 4. An article by Professor Patwardhan, on "Tukārām's Doctrine of *Bhakti*," was published in the *Indian Interpreter*, Vol. VII, No. 1; and in the same magazine, Vol. VII, No. 4, Rev. D. Mackichan, D.D., LL.D., writes on "The Marāṭhās and Their Literature." A chapter of Sir R. G. Bhandarkar's *Vaiṣṇāvism, Śaivism, and Minor Religious Systems* (Encyclopædia of Indo-Aryan Research) is devoted to Nāmdev and Tukārām, and gives a number of translations of their *abhaṅgs*. Reference may also be made to the "Notes" prefixed to Molesworth's Marāṭhī Dictionary by Dr. John Wilson, and to contributions by Dr. Murray Mitchell in the *Transactions of the Bombay Branch of the Royal Asiatic Society*, Vol. III (1849) and in the *Transactions of the Congress of Orientalists*, 1892.

For an account of these saints in their relation to the historical situation of their times, see M. G. Ramade's *Rise of the Maratha Power*, Chapter VIII. See also *Tales of the Saints of Paṇḍharpūr*, by C. A. Kincard, (Oxford University Press, 1919).

The poems of Tukārām have been translated into English prose by J. Nelson Fraser and K. B. Marathe, 3 Vols., Christian Literature Society, Madras (1909-15).

I

INDEX

ABHANG 11, 14, 16, 26, 34
Advaita 21, 25, 26, 68, 80, 89
Akrūra 52, 53
Ālandī 14
Amṛit Anubhāv 14, 15
Arjuna 52, 53
Arnold, Matthew 30

BALĪ 52, 53
Benares 20
Bhagavadgītā 14
Bhāgvata Purāṇa 51
Bhajan 12, 40
Bhakti 21, 24, 32, 52, 53, 81, 89
Bhandarkar, Sir R. G. 15, 18
Bhāvārtha Rāmāyaṇa 53
Bhīmā 11, 54
Bhūpati 52, 53
Brahman 17, 24, 25, 30, 38, 42, 68, 82, 89

CAITANYA 19, 22
Cokā Melā 23

DEHŪ 19, 20, 59
Dharma 35, 85

ECKHART 27
Ekanāth 12, 23, 51-55

GANGES 20, 54, 81
Godaverī 23
Govind 48, 90

HARI 38, 72
Haridās 12, 45
Hebrew Psalmists 27, 28, 29, 31, 32
Hṛiṣikeśa 43

INDRĀYANI 20

JANĀBĀĪ 16, 17, 49, 50
Janārdan 54
Jñāndev } 12, 13-15, 19, 22, 24
Jñāneśvar } 25, 35-40, 41
Jñāneśvarī 13, 14, 15, 35-38

KABĪR 22, 25, 26
Kamalā 44
Karhād 15
Keśav 17, 44, 73, 74
Keśav Caitanya 19
Kīrtan 12, 81
Kṛiṣṇa 11, 24, 35, 44, 45, 84

MĀDHAV 40
Mahār 23
Māruti 52, 53
Māyā 17
Mount Meru 17, 37
Muhammadanism 18, 31
Muktābāī 14, 41, 42
Mukti, Mokṣa 35, 83
Mutiny 31

NĀGNĀTH 16
Nāmdev 13, 15-18, 24, 42-48
Nārāyaṇa 58, 60, 62, 67, 80
Nivṛittināth 14, 42

PAITHAN 23
Pāṇḍav 36
Paṇḍharī } 11, 18, 23, 44, 57,
Paṇḍharpūr } 76
Prahlād 39, 52, 53
Puṇḍlik 49
Purāṇās 45

RĀGHAV Caitanya 19
Rāma 52, 53
Ranade, M. G. 12, 15, 18
Rāmānanda 22
Release 35, 68, 69
Rukmiṇī, Rakhumāī } 40, 45

ŚAṄKARĀCĀRYA 25
Senā 55
Siṁhasth 88
Śivājī 18
Sopāndev 14, 42
Śrī Śuka 52, 53

TAGORE, Sir Rabindranath 26

Tukārām 12, 13, 18-21, 23, 25, 28, 30, 31, 32, 33, 56-90

UDDHAV 39, 51

VAIKUṆṬHA 20, 64, 85
Vāsudev 47
Vedānt 24
Viṣṇu 11
Viṭhobā, Viṭṭhal } 11, 15, 16, 19, 23 40, 44, 49, 50, 57, 60, 62, 65, 66, 72
Vyāsa 39

YAMA 90
Yoga, Yogī 36, 39, 73, 77

II

INDEX OF TRANSLATIONS

JNĀNEŚVAR

Jñāneśvarī ix, 188ff., p. 35
Do. ix, 197ff., p. 36
Do. xii, 197ff., p. 37
Do. xvi, 114ff., p. 37
Abhaṅgs, pp. 38-40

MUKTĀBĀĪ

Abhaṅgs, p. 41

NĀMDEV

Abhaṅgs :
Āvaṭe 198, p. 50 ; do. 207, p. 46 ; do. 333, p. 44 ; do. 351, p. 44 ; do. 358, p. 42 ; do. 391, p. 45 ; do. 501, p. 44 ; do. 583, p. 47 ; do. 586; p. 48 ; do. 938, p. 42 ; do, 416, p. 47 ; do. 1449, p. 46. do. 1482, p. 43

EKANĀTH

Bhāgavat, xi, 1458ff., p. 51
Bhāvārtha Rāmāyaṇa, Chap. i, p. 53
Abhaṅgs, pp. 52, 54-55

SENA

Abhaṅg, p. 55.

TUKĀRĀM

Abhaṅgs: I.P. 90, p. 89 ; do. 109, p. 83 ; do. 260, p. 85 ; do. 266, p. 56 ; do. 300, p. 85 ; do. 347, p. 79 ; do. 469, p. 58 ; do. 502, p. 57 ; do. 520, p. 85 ; do. 530, p. 56 ; do. 580, p. 80 ; do. 602, p. 74 ; do. 603, p. 90 ; do. 626, p. 69 ; do. 648, p. 68 ; do. 702, p. 70 ; do. 716, p. 75 ; do. 758, p. 75 ; do. 764, p. 76 ; do. 776, p. 90 ; do. 783, p. 72 ; do. 806, p. 62 ; do. 801, p. 73 ; do. 818, p. 71 ; do. 819, p. 75 ; do. 827, p. 58 ; do. 868, p. 62 ; do. 948, p. 88 ; do. 949, p. 83 ; do. 977, p. 78 ; do. 1001, p. 76 ; do. 1031, p. 63 ; do. 1033, p. 70 ; do. 1368, p. 84 ; do. 1436, p. 80 ; do. 1437, p. 72 ; do. 1462, p. 83 ; do. 1471, p. 89 ; do. 1482, p. 89 ; do. 1540, p. 62 ; do. 1562, p. 86; do. 1589, p. 81 ; do. 1779, p. 76 ; do. 1820, p. 57 ; do. 1836, p. 59 ; do. 1870, p. 73; do. 1996, p. 64 ; do. 2000, p. 71 ; do. 2051, p. 81 ; do. 2341, p. 81 ; do. 2638, p. 74; do. 2668, p. 79 ; do. 2672, p. 64 ; do. 2693, p. 87 ; do. 2811, p. 86 ; do. 2824, p. 60 ; do. 2849, p. 77 ; do. 2869, p. 88 ; do. 2949, p. 88 ; do. 2966, p. 77 ; do. 3189, p. 82 ; do. 3443, p. 64 ; do. 3474, p. 79 ; do. 3653, p. 61 ; do. 3695, p. 65 ; do. 3696, p. 78 ; do. 3753, p. 68 ; do. 3837, p. 66 ; do. 4004, p. 65 ; do. 4161, p. 70 ; do. 4265, p. 82 ; do. 4361, p. 67 : do. 4381, p. 61 ; do. 4419, p. 66 ; do. 4420, p. 67

An *abhaṅg* not in the Indu Prakāś collection is translated on p. 87